Harvard Business Review

ON

DEVELOPING HIGH-POTENTIAL LEADERS

THE HARVARD BUSINESS REVIEW PAPERBACK SERIES

The series is designed to bring today's managers and professionals the fundamental information they need to stay competitive in a fast-moving world. From the preeminent thinkers whose work has defined an entire field to the rising stars who will redefine the way we think about business, here are the leading minds and landmark ideas that have established the *Harvard Business Review* as required reading for ambitious businesspeople in organizations around the globe.

Other books in the series:

Harvard Business Review Interviews with CEOs

Harvard Business Review on Advances in Strategy

Harvard Business Review on Appraising Employee Performance

Harvard Business Review on Becoming a High Performance Manager

Harvard Business Review on Brand Management

Harvard Business Review on Breakthrough Leadership

Harvard Business Review on Breakthrough Thinking

Harvard Business Review on Bringing Your Whole Self to Work

Harvard Business Review on Building Personal and Organizational Resilience

Harvard Business Review on the Business Value of IT

Harvard Business Review on Change

Harvard Business Review on Collaborating Across Silos

Harvard Business Review on Compensation

Harvard Business Review on Corporate Ethics

Harvard Business Review on Corporate Governance

Harvard Business Review on Corporate Responsibility

Harvard Business Review on Corporate Strategy

Harvard Business Review on Crisis Management

Harvard Business Review on Culture and Change

Other books in the series (continued):

Harvard Business Review on Customer Relationship Management
Harvard Business Review on Decision Making
Harvard Business Review on Developing Leaders
Harvard Business Review on Doing Business in China
Harvard Business Review on Effective Communication
Harvard Business Review on Entrepreneurship
Harvard Business Review on Finding and Keeping the Best People
Harvard Business Review on Green Business Strategy
Harvard Business Review on the High-Performance Organization
Harvard Business Review on Innovation
Harvard Business Review on the Innovative Enterprise
Harvard Business Review on Knowledge Management
Harvard Business Review on Leadership
Harvard Business Review on Leadership at the Top
Harvard Business Review on Leadership in a Changed World
Harvard Business Review on Leading in Turbulent Times
Harvard Business Review on Leading Through Change
Harvard Business Review on Making Smarter Decisions
Harvard Business Review on Managing Diversity
Harvard Business Review on Managing External Risk
Harvard Business Review on Managing Health Care
Harvard Business Review on Managing High-Tech Industries
Harvard Business Review on Managing People
Harvard Business Review on Managing Projects
Harvard Business Review on Managing Through a Downturn
Harvard Business Review on Managing Uncertainty
Harvard Business Review on Managing the Value Chain
Harvard Business Review on Managing Your Career
Harvard Business Review on Managing Yourself
Harvard Business Review on Marketing

Other books in the series (continued):

Harvard Business Review on Measuring Corporate Performance

Harvard Business Review on Mergers and Acquisitions

Harvard Business Review on the Mind of the Leader

Harvard Business Review on Motivating People

Harvard Business Review on Negotiation and Conflict Resolution

Harvard Business Review on Nonprofits

Harvard Business Review on Organizational Learning

Harvard Business Review on the Persuasive Leader

Harvard Business Review on Profiting from Green Business

Harvard Business Review on Strategic Alliances

Harvard Business Review on Strategic Renewal

Harvard Business Review on Strategic Sales Management

Harvard Business Review on Strategies for Growth

Harvard Business Review on Supply-Chain Management

Harvard Business Review on Talent Management

Harvard Business Review on Teams That Succeed

Harvard Business Review on the Tests of a Leader

Harvard Business Review on Top-Line Growth

Harvard Business Review on Turnarounds

Harvard Business Review on Women in Business

Harvard Business Review on Work and Life Balance

Harvard Business Review

ON

DEVELOPING

HIGH-POTENTIAL LEADERS

A HARVARD BUSINESS REVIEW PAPERBACK

Printed in the United States of America
13 12 11 10 09 5 4 3 2 1

Library of Congress Cataloging-in-Publication Data

Harvard business review on developing high-potential leaders.
p. cm.
Includes index.
ISBN 978-1-4221-2870-1 (pbk.)
1. Executive ability. 2. Executives—Training of. 3. Leadership.
I. Harvard business review. II. Title: On developing high-potential leaders.
HD38.2.H37434 2009
658.4'092—dc22

2009010443

Table of Contents

Harvard Business Review

ON

DEVELOPING HIGH-POTENTIAL LEADERS

When a New Manager Takes Charge

JOHN J. GABARRO

Executive Summary

WHEN SOME MANAGERS take over a new job, they hit the ground running. They learn the ropes, get along with their bosses and subordinates, gain credibility, and ultimately master the situation. Others, however, don't do so well. What accounts for the difference?

In this article, first published in 1985, Harvard Business School professor John J. Gabarro relates the findings of two sets of field studies he conducted, covering 14 management successions. The first set was a three-year study of four newly assigned division presidents; the second consisted of ten historical case studies. The project comprised American and European organizations with sales varying from $1.2 million to $3 billion. It included turnarounds, normal situations, failures, and triumphs.

According to the author, the taking-charge process follows five predictable stages: taking hold, immersion, reshaping, consolidation, and refinement. These phases are characterized by a series of alternating periods of intense learning (immersion and refinement) and action (taking hold, reshaping, and consolidation). The study's results put to rest the myth of the all-purpose general manager who can be dropped into any situation and emerge triumphant. Understanding a situation and effecting change do not occur overnight, says Gabarro, and human variables such as managerial styles and effective working relationships make a difference.

Editor's Note: A great deal has been written about first managerial jobs and their attendant woes; similarly, there are whole shelves of books devoted to the art and science of becoming a CEO. Fewer publications address what happens when general managers take over a division or function in large organizations. Yet these are the transitions through which a manager becomes—or fails to become—a leader.

More than 20 years ago, Harvard Business School professor John J. Gabarro conducted a research project to examine what happens when general managers take on big new jobs. The project consisted of a three-year longitudinal study followed by a set of ten historical case studies of management successions. Specifically, Gabarro was trying to sort out why some managers failed but others succeeded. In this 1985 article, he reported on his findings: Managers took much longer than predicted to get up to speed; successful transitions followed predictable stages (including two sit-back-and-watch periods of immersion and refinement); industry insiders took charge much faster than outsiders; and a good working relationship with a boss dramatically increased the likelihood of success. Gabarro's most important finding overall was that taking charge takes a long, long time. Given the now common practice of shortened general-management assignments, are organizations paying a huge, hidden cost?

THE SUBSIDIARY WAS IN SERIOUS trouble, so top management hired a young vice president of marketing with an enviable track record in another industry and gave him carte blanche. He reorganized the marketing function using a brand management concept, restructured the sales division, and devised new marketing strategies. Margins continued to erode, however, and after nine months he lost his job.

In another company, top management also hired a manager from a different industry to turn around a subsidiary's heavy losses and gave him considerable latitude. He too formulated an entirely new marketing strategy along brand lines. Within a year's time, margins improved, and within three years the subsidiary was very profitable and sales had doubled.

On the surface, these two situations are strikingly similar. Both executives were in their middle thirties, and neither had experience in his new industry. The two men implemented major changes that were remarkably alike. Furthermore, both worked for difficult bosses. Yet one succeeded and the other failed. What factors account for the different outcomes?

To answer this question, we need to look deeper and explore the contexts the two managers faced, their backgrounds, and the taking-charge process itself.

Although only dramatic examples make headlines, a recent study shows that by the time general managers reach their late forties, they have already taken charge of three to nine management posts.[1] Despite the frequency, however, and because situations are unique and managers so different, it is difficult to generalize about the taking-charge process.

Having studied 14 management successions, though, I have found issues common to all and factors that not only affect them but also influence how successful a new person is likely to be. (See the exhibit "The Managers Taking Charge," which details the research process.)

In using the term *taking charge,* I am referring to the process of learning and taking action that a manager goes through until he (or she) has mastered a new assignment in sufficient depth to be running the organization as well as resources and constraints allow.

The taking-charge process occurs in several predictable stages, each of which has its own tasks, problems, and dilemmas. My study's findings also put to rest the myth of the all-purpose general manager who can be dropped into any situation and triumph. To the contrary, my observations indicate that managers' experiences have a profound and inescapable influence on how they

The Managers Taking Charge

This article is based on a research project that consisted of two sets of field studies totaling 14 management successions. The first set was a longitudinal study of four newly assigned division presidents whom I studied over a three-year period as they went about the process of taking charge. The second set consisted of ten historical case studies of management successions, which were used to expand on and verify the longitudinal studies' results. The 14 cases were chosen to get a range of different kinds of management successions involving both functional and general managers. The successions included American and European organizations varying in sales from $1.2 million to $3 billion. The sample included turnarounds and normal situations and successions that failed as well as those that succeeded.

I studied the longitudinal cases using company documents, on-site observation, and field interviews with the new presidents and their subordinates at the end of three, six, 12, 15, 18, 24, 27, 30, and 36 months. For the historical studies, field interviews were conducted and company documents were used.

Summary description of managers studied

Unit's business	Unit revenues*	Manager's job	Predecessor as superior	Turnaround situation	Industry-specfic experience	Insider (I) or outsider (O) to organization	Location	Succession success (S) or failure (F)†
Longitudinal case studies								
Industrial and office products division	$260 million	Division president	yes	no	yes	I	U.S.	S

Summary description of managers studied

Unit's business	Unit revenues*	Manager's job	Predecessor as superior	Turnaround situation	Industry-specfic experience	Insider (I) or outsider (O) to organization	Location	Succession success (S) or failure (F)†
Longitudinal case studies								
Machine tool division	175 million	Division president	no	yes	no	O	U.S.	S
Consumer products division	70 million	Division president	no	yes	no	O	U.S.	S
Construction products division	55 million	Division president	yes	no	no	O	U.S.	S
Historical case studies								
Cable television subsidiary	$1.2 million	General manager	no	no	no	O	U.S.	F
Wholesale food distributor	21 million	Functional head	no	yes	no	O	U.S.	F
District sales organization (communications)	30 million	Functional head	no	no	yes	I	U.S.	S

Beverage manufacturer	90 million	General manager	no	yes	no	O	Netherlands	S
Plastic and metal products	100 million	General manager	yes	no	yes	I	UK	F
Beverage manufacturer	110 million	Functional head	yes	no	no	O	Italy	F
Synthetic fibers	200 million	Functional head	yes	yes	yes	I	UK	S
Computer and technical products	780 million	General manager	no	no	yes	I	Switzerland	S
Industrial and consumer products	3 billion	General manager	no	yes	yes	I	UK	S
Public education	Not available	Functional manager	no	yes	yes	I	U.S.	S

* Unit revenues expressed in 1982 U.S. dollars.

† A succession was considered a failure if the new manager was fired within the first 36 months because of his inability to meet top management's expectations of performance.

take charge, what areas they focus on, and how successful they are likely to be in mastering the new situation.

The New Manager Arrives

When I looked at the taking-charge process for a period of time, two patterns stood out. First, the process can be long. In the cases studied, for senior U.S. managers, it took from two to two and a half years; some European and UK senior managers took even longer. Second, the taking-charge process does not involve steadily more learning or action. Rather, it is a series of alternating phases of intense learning and intense action. Also, the nature of both the managers' learning and actions changes over time.

With few exceptions, most new managers' organizational changes tended to cluster in three bursts of activity. Exhibit I shows these periods quite clearly. Exhibit II illustrates that the same bursts occur regardless of the type of succession. The data presented in Exhibits I, II, III, and IV are for completed successions only, in other words, those in which the new manager lasted in the job for two and a half years or longer. As such, the exhibits do not include data from three of the failed successions. The organizational activity measure is a composite of both structural and personnel changes managers made.

What accounts for this pervasive pattern? Why were the major changes made almost invariably in three waves of action? My observations suggest that the underlying patterns of learning and action account for these periods of intense change. They are natural consequences of how new managers learn and act as they try to master strange situations. More specifically, the data

Exhibit I: Average Number of Organizational Changes per Three-Month Period Following Succession

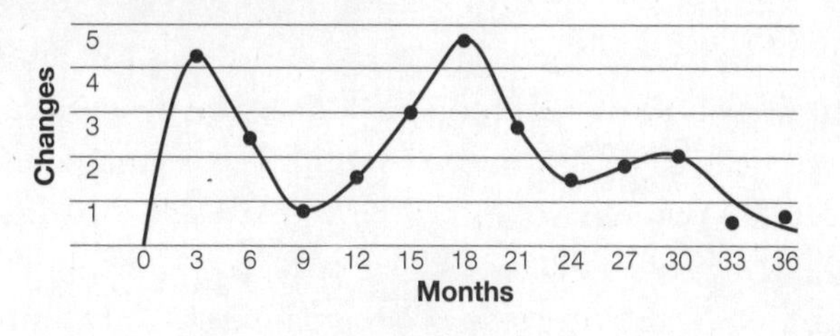

Exhibit II: Average Number of Organizational Changes per Six-Month Period Following Succession, Categorized

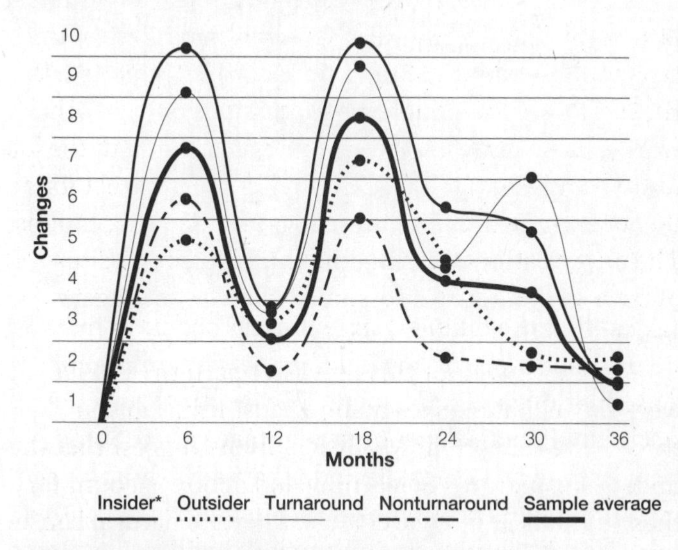

*Insider successions are those in which the new manager had five or more years' experience in the new organization's industry.

Exhibit III: Personnel and Structural Changes Made (by six-month periods)

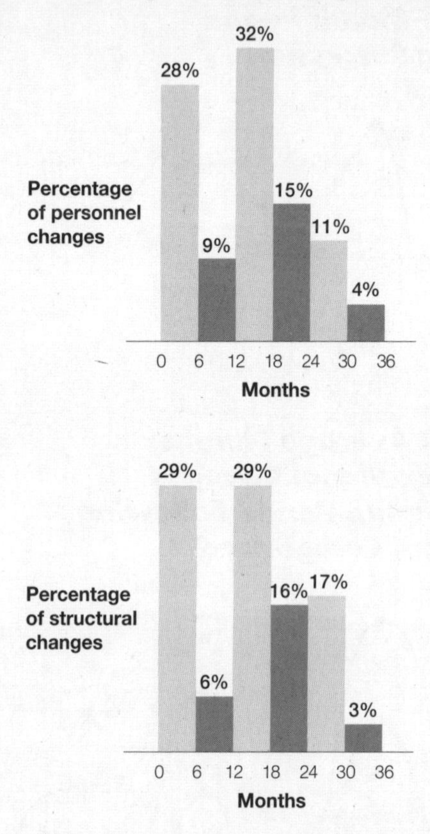

suggest that the taking-charge process occurs in five predictable stages: taking hold, immersion, reshaping, consolidation, and refinement. The length of time the executives I studied spent in each stage varied. Some spent as long as 11 months and others as little as four in the same stage. Thus, time doesn't define a stage; rather, the nature of learning and the action that characterizes it does. Let's look at each stage more carefully.

Exhibit IV: Summary of How Managers' Functional Experience Affected Their Actions

		Longitudinal studies				Historical studies									
		Division presidents				Other general managers					Functional managers				
		1	2	3	4	5	6	7	8	9	10	11	12	13	14
Actions taken	**Initial actions** Initial activities were in area of prior functional experience.	X	X	X	X	X	X	X	X	X	X	X	NO	X	X
	First structural change affected area of prior functional experience.	X	X	X	X	X	NO	NA	X	X	X	NA	NO	X	NA
	Major action Most significant change made in first three years affected area of prior functional experience.	X	X	X	X	X	X	X	X	X	X	X	NO	X	X
	Most significant structural change affected area of prior functional experience.	X	X	X	X	X	X	NA	X	X	X	NA	X	X	NA

X = yes
NO = no
NA = not available

TAKING HOLD

The first stage, taking hold, typically lasts from three to six months and often sets the tone, if not the direction, for the rest of the taking-charge process. (Exhibit III shows the percentages of personnel and structural changes by six-month periods, which the managers made during their successions.) Taking hold is a period of intense action and learning. If the new assignment is a big promotion or change, the newcomer may at times feel overwhelmed. A new division president commented: "You're on the edge of your seat all the time. It feels like you have no knowledge base whatsoever. You have to learn the product, the people, and the problems. You're trying like hell to learn about the organization and the people awfully fast, and that's the trickiest thing. At first you're afraid to do anything for fear of upsetting the apple cart. The problem is you have to keep the business running while you're learning about it."

During this period, a manager is grappling with the nature of the new situation, trying to understand the tasks and problems and assessing the organization and its requirements. Managers orient themselves, evaluate the situation, and develop a cognitive map. For example, one division president who was an industry outsider described his learning task as so large that even locking himself up for four days to review strategic, financial, marketing, and industry reports barely made a dent. Early in this stage, he also reported that it took him several hours to go through the morning mail, not only because the issues were new to him but also because the industry had its own technical jargon and nomenclature. Another manager in a similar situation voiced his exasperation by saying resignedly, "There aren't enough hours in the day." (All of the managers in the study happened to be men. I have every reason to believe that female managers would go through the same stages.)

Evaluation and orientation in the taking-hold stage are important even for insiders who already know of the organization and the product. A division president with more than 25 years in his organization spent the first three months in his new job testing his assumptions about key people and the division's problems. He came to several conclusions, one of which was that a senior vice president in his group was in over his head. The division president based his assessment on a number of meetings with the senior vice president, his subordinates' opinions, his plan for the previous five years, complaints about cliques in his area, problems with division functions, and the senior VP's insensitive treatment of two of the company's major overseas distributors. The last item was particularly troublesome because it made the new president doubt the man's judgment. Questioning previous perceptions and beliefs characterized most insider successions during this stage.

Actions taken during the taking-hold stage tend to be corrective. Based on their experience and what they have learned about the new situation, managers fix what problems they can. Obviously, corrective actions vary—some are short-term interventions, others take longer. For instance, in one case, although it took nearly five months before the new manager had developed a strategy for turning around the division, because of his experience, within a month he knew that the division needed both a cost system and a product-line reduction immediately.

A group CEO approached this stage quite differently, however. Having been promoted from within and having himself previously turned around the business's manufacturing operation, he did not make significant short-term corrections his first priority. Rather, focusing on product strategy and planning, he established committees and teams to address these areas. Although his actions did not have the same fix-it quality of the other turnaround, they were nonetheless corrective in that they dealt with areas the new CEO considered critical to the group's success.

The magnitude of corrective action also varies. In his third month in office, a division president with 25 years of experience in the company reorganized his new area. In contrast, the division presidents who were outsiders did not implement comparable changes until their second year in office, when they were well beyond the taking-hold stage.

IMMERSION

Compared with the taking-hold stage, the immersion period is quiet. Exhibit III shows a dramatic decrease in changes after the first six months: Only 6% of organizational and 9% of personnel changes occurred during the second six months, a time period that generally coincided with the beginning of the immersion phase. A lull between bursts of activity, immersion is a very significant time, however, during which executives acquire greater understanding of their new situations. In the U.S. cases I studied, this stage lasted four to 11 months.

During immersion, new managers run the organization in a more informed fashion and steep themselves in a less hectic, finer-grained learning process than was possible when they were taking hold. Consequently, by the end of this stage, they have developed a new concept or at least have greatly revised their ideas of what they need to do.

More focused learning happens during this period because managers immerse themselves in running the organization, and they learn from the interactions and conflicts they deal with day to day. As their experience base grows, they can see patterns they didn't see before. In one case, for example, even though the new division manager made several momentous changes—reorganizing manufacturing by product lines and implementing better control, scheduling, and cost systems—during the taking-hold stage, manufacturing cost problems persisted. During the immersion stage, he was able to see that many of these had their roots in the product's design and, ultimately, in how the division's engineering group was structured. It took, however, six to eight months of exploration before this underlying cause became clear.

Even when changes made in the taking-hold stage work, the immersion period still offers opportunities for further learning. New problems that had been masked or overshadowed by larger problems emerge. For example, after a division president had reorganized his division from a functional to a geographic structure, with a domestic-international split, a new set of problems surfaced during the immersion period that neither he nor his management team had foreseen. The earlier reorganization significantly increased the responsiveness, productivity, and coordination between functions in the United States and abroad, but as these areas improved, the U.S. sales force's organization and its distribution channels showed weaknesses. The old structure's cross-functional problems had hidden these weaknesses.

During immersion, new managers also question whether they have the right people in place. Obvious questions about competence arose in the taking-hold stage, but now they were easier to discern. Similarly, in more than half the cases studied, the newcomers explored uncertainties they had about staff members and discussed them with others.

The analysis, probes, discussions, and, in some cases, agony of the immersion stage result in new managers' arriving at a better understanding of the more basic dynamics of the organization, people, and the industry. The concept that emerges from this stage (whether new or refined) is not necessarily radical. In six of the 14 cases, however, the revised concept had implications for radical changes in either strategy or organization or both. In most of the cases, it also resulted in a sharper plan of action for improving the situation further.

RESHAPING

During the third stage, reshaping, the second important—and in most cases the largest—burst of activity takes place. Learning continues but in a more diminished and routine fashion. In the reshaping period, new managers direct their attention toward reconfiguring one or more aspects of the organization to implement the concept they developed or made final during the immersion stage.

The reshaping stage, like the taking-hold period, involves a great deal of organizational change. Exhibit III shows that more than 32% of the personnel changes and 29% of the structural changes were made during the third six-month period. Again I should caution that the stages did not neatly apportion themselves out into six-month periods. Nonetheless, after 13 to 18 months, most managers studied had reached the reshaping stage, where they were eager to act on the learning and exploration they had experienced in the immersion period. Indeed, immersion activities usually pave the way for reshaping-stage changes.

Immersion is a transition, and by the end of it, new managers and often their key subordinates are impatient to get on with things. In one case, for example, a new division president had to fend off growing pressure from two of his vice presidents while he commissioned several task forces to focus on the areas of intended change. As he put it, "The task force reports will take us to the point where there will be no surprises and a lot of added insights. The nice part of this is that everyone will know what needs to be done, and they'll have ownership of the changes we decide to make. If the obvious answer is wrong, the reports will flush it out. In the meantime, I have to convince the guys down the hall that the added time this requires is worth it."

Reshaping-stage changes may involve altering processes as well as making major structural shifts. Two divisions studied went from product to functional structures.

As one would imagine, the reshaping stage is very busy, especially if it involves major changes. For example, when one manager was reorganizing both marketing and sales, he had to call two series of meetings (one with the affected managers and another with the district sales forces to explain the changes), work out details where positional changes and relocations were involved, and call on key customers and distributors. Thus, although management announced plans for the changes at the outset of this stage, their implementation took nearly eight weeks of sustained activity on the part of the new president, his new marketing VP, and his domestic sales manager. As one would expect, the learning in the reshaping stage consists mainly of feedback, for example, on the impact the sales reorganization had on key distributors and on orders.

Reshaping ends when new managers have implemented as much of their concept as circumstances allow. In practice, several factors (the most common is the unavailability of people for key positions) often prevent them from completing the job.

CONSOLIDATION

The third and final wave of action in the taking-charge process occurs during the fourth stage, consolidation. Throughout this period, much of new managers' learning and action focuses on consolidating and following through on the changes they made during reshaping. The process is evaluative; for example, new managers and their key subordinates judge the consequences of the actions they took in the reshaping burst of activity and take corrective measures.

Learning at this point involves two sets of issues, the first of which is identifying what the leftover follow-through implementation problems are and how to deal with them. For instance, during his reshaping stage, a new president had reorganized his division from a product to a functional structure. But he had deferred integrating one of the former product group's manufacturing departments into the divisional manufacturing function until several other changes had been completed. When most of the reorganization had been accomplished, he and his manufacturing vice president began to study how the product group could be integrated.

A second set of issues evolves from unanticipated problems resulting from changes made during the reshaping stage. Much of the consolidation period's extraordinary activity involves diagnosing and studying these problems, then correcting them.

Finally, during consolidation, new managers deal with those aspects of their concept that they could not implement before. In several situations, for instance, managers had to wait to find a person for an important position or to transfer one of the organization's managers who could not move earlier.

REFINEMENT

The refinement stage is a period of little organizational change. By this point, executives have taken charge, and their learning and actions tend to focus either on refining operations or on looking for opportunities in the marketplace, in technology, or in other areas. In one case, the manager looked at potential acquisitions; in another, the manager seriously considered divesting part of the business.

This stage marks the end of the taking-charge process. By this time managers can no longer be considered new. They no longer feel new, nor do their subordinates perceive or speak of them as new. Whatever the problems the executives now face, they do not result from newness. By now, they have either established credibility and a power base, or they have not. They have had enough time to shape their situations, and they will be judged by the results of their actions. If they are still uncomfortable, usually it is because of pressing business problems such as a recession or mounting interest rates rather than unfamiliarity with their jobs.

Refinement is a calm period. From this stage onward, managers' learning will be more incremental and routine. Important developments in the economy, the marketplace, or technology may destroy this calmness, but whatever additional learning and action such factors lead to, they do not result from newness. For better or worse, the manager has taken charge.

What Makes a Difference?

A number of factors shape how executives progress through these stages and how successfully they take charge. Important determinants include a new manager's experience, whether the business needs turning around, the person's managerial style and personal needs, his relationships with key people by the end of the first year, and whether the manager's management style conflicts with that of his boss. Let me describe each of these in more detail.

ROOTS THAT ENDURE

All other things being equal, managers' functional backgrounds, managerial experiences, and special competencies appear to determine how they take charge: what actions they take and how competently they implement them.

The extent to which managers' functional experience influences their actions is quite surprising. For 13 of the 14 new managers studied, their initial actions were in areas where they had had functional experience, and the most significant changes they made during the three years also were in the areas where they had experience (see Exhibit IV). This pattern is not surprising for functional managers. But emergence of the same pattern among the general managers reveals the extent to which experience influences actions and points of view.

Because Exhibit IV is a summary, it under-states both the specificity and pervasiveness of how much the new managers' experience affected their actions. Exhibit V looks at ten managers' experience and actions in some detail.

If one thinks in terms of the five taking-charge stages, this pattern is not so surprising. Indeed, one could predict that any significant additional experience base managers gain as a result of taking charge of a new assignment will not be firm until after they have experienced the deeper learning of the immersion stage, acted on this knowledge in the reshaping stage, and learned from these actions in the consolidation stage.

Insiders versus outsiders. New managers' experience in their organization's industry also affected significantly how they took charge and what problems they encountered. First, industry insiders (managers who have five or more years' experience in the new organization's industry) take hold much more quickly than do outsiders. Insiders begin with a larger wave of action and their actions tend to be more basic. For example, fully 33% of all of the structural changes industry insiders made occurred during their first six months. Second, the number of actions insiders take is greater not only in the taking-hold stage (in the study, on average, insiders' actions were twice as frequent) but throughout the entire taking-charge process. Moreover, whereas three of four of the managers who did not succeed in their jobs lacked industry experience, only four of ten successful managers

Exhibit V: Comparison of Managers' Functional Experience and Actions Taken (historical studies)

Business, manager's title, and company sales	Prior assignment	Functional experience	Initial area of major involvement	Areas affected by first structural change	Areas affected by major structural change	Areas affected by most significant changes of first three years
Cable television subsidiary General manager $1.2 million	Communications engineer (in another company)	Engineering	Construction and engineering Planning	Engineering installation and construction	Same	Reorganization of chief engineer's department affecting engineering, construction, and installation
Wholesale food distribution Vice president–marketing and sales $21 million	Vice president-marketing and planning (in another company)	Marketing and product management	Product planning and reduction of sales force	Creation of product manager's position and reorganization of product sales groups	Marketing (creation of product manager's responsibilities)	Introduction of product management
District sales service organization District manager $30 million	Sales service administrator (in same company)	Customer service	Sales service audit	(No structural changes made)	(No structural changes made)	Sales service training
Beverage manufacturer Division general manager $80 million	Division general manager (in another company)	Marketing and market planning (also experience in two prior turnarounds as general manager)	Sales force and marketing	Sales force	Creation of marketing function and reorganization of sales force	Revision of mission scope and revamping of marketing strategy affecting marketing and sales

Plastic and metal products Group managing director $100 million	Division general manager (in same company)	Manufacturing and engineering	Manufacturing rationalization	(No structural changes made)	(No structural changes made)	Manufacturing rationalization
Beverage manufacturer Director of marketing and sales $110 million	Marketing and sales director (in another company)	Marketing	Sales and sales procedures and information systems	Sales force	Sales and marketing	Sales systems and procedures
Synthetic fibers Director of manufacturing $300 million	Works manager (in same company)	Manufacturing and engineering	Restructuring of manufacturing management	Manufacturing	Same	Rationalization and restructuring of production operations
Computer and technical products Group vice president and general manager $780 million	Group general marketing manager (in same company)	Marketing, sales operations, and engineering	Marketing and sales operations	Group staff functions (finance, controller, group support functions)	Sales operations and marketing	Restructuring of sales operations
Industrial and consumer Group CEO $3 billion	Group manufacturing director (in same company)	Manufacturing management and production control (turnaround experience)	Product strategy and product planning, manufacturing operations, and production engineering	Manufacturing and production engineering	Manufacturing, product engineering, and product planning	Manufacturing operations, production engineering, quality control, and product planning
Public education Administrator	Administrator (in same system)	Educational administration (turnaround experience)	School discipline, athletics and activities, accreditation, and community involvement	(Not applicable)	(Not applicable)	Discipline, academic standards, student activities, and community involvement

lacked such experience (I defined a failed appointment as one in which the new manager was fired within three years of taking charge).

One case, in which a marketing manager with more than 15 years' experience in packaged goods and toiletries became marketing and sales director of a $110 million beverage division, illustrates an outsider's difficulties. On the surface, his background looked like a good fit, but the new industry was different from traditional packaged goods in a number of important ways. The outsider's experience had served him well in product planning and changing systems during the taking-hold period and later in restructuring the sales force. It had not, however, prepared him for dealing with the sales force or his major distributors, both of which required a hands-on approach. By the end of the taking-hold stage, he was in serious trouble with both groups. By the end of his first year, his cool, professional, managerial style had alienated some key distributors so much that the division general manager had to intervene in several critical situations. These incidents undermined the new manager's ability to develop credibility with customers and subordinates.

TURNING THINGS AROUND

How unfavorable a new situation was also influenced the taking-charge process in the cases I studied. In turnarounds managers feel a great deal of pressure to act on problems quickly. One might expect that in a turnaround, because of the urgency of the situation, executives would have a shorter taking-hold stage, but neither the aggregated data nor the individual case data support this. If anything, the data suggest that the taking-hold wave actually lasts longer in a turnaround.

Although the action waves are of comparable duration, the activity in the reshaping and consolidation stages peaks earlier in the turnarounds by about three to six months, a pattern which no doubt reflects the urgency experienced in turnarounds.

None of these differences between normal successions and turnarounds that the data uncovered is surprising. Others, which surfaced in manager interviews, are. For one thing, turnaround managers told me they knew they would have to redo later some of the changes they were making in the taking-hold stage.

In one case, the new general manager reported he knew from experience (this was his third turnaround) that it would take five to six months to design and implement a cost system that was sophisticated enough to provide all the information he needed on which products were losing money and why. He concluded that he simply did not have the time to do it perfectly and opted instead for a system that would give him, as quickly as possible, a better vision of the problems.

Managers don't make such suboptimal decisions gladly. When new managers and their subordinates had fewer problems to deal with (usually in the consolidation period), they would go back and improve the tourniquet systems and processes they had installed earlier.

Although the turnaround managers were under much greater pressure than their non-turnaround counterparts, they benefited from certain advantages. Generally speaking, their companies gave them much more latitude in taking action than the managers had in the normal successions. This was particularly true during the taking-hold stage. The two situations I described in the beginning of the article illustrate this well.

In the first case, after six weeks on the job, the new marketing vice president proposed a wholly new marketing strategy that top management rapidly approved. Such agreeableness is rare in nonturnaround successions. In the second case, the new manager's head office not only gave him a much greater degree of freedom than it usually gave its division general managers, but it also buffered him from corporate staff intervention for the first two years. After the manager completed the turnaround, top management told him he now had to play by the rules and conform more closely to corporate policies.

Generally, because of the urgency of the situations, the turnaround managers started with a larger power base than their counterparts and faced less rivalry from key subordinates who might have wanted their jobs. But several turnaround managers reported feeling their organizations were fearful and tense, which put additional pressure on them to settle things as quickly as possible.

THE NEW MANAGER'S STYLE

The 14 men I studied varied significantly in their styles, including how they spent their time—alone, in meetings, on tours—what kinds of meetings and interactions they preferred—one-to-one, recurrently scheduled or specially scheduled meetings, planned meetings versus ad hoc meetings—and their preferences for formality or informality.

Managerial style affects how people respond to an executive initially and influences the entire taking-charge process, including how the person makes decisions. The most dramatic example of this was one president who had a fairly hands-on approach to problems and needed control. Because he thought that the product organization prevented him from seeing problems at the functional level, he struggled throughout the immersion stage. Finally, he reorganized the division from a product to a functional structure. The implementation of this change was painful for the organization and required that several functional vice presidents split their time among three businesses, two of which were geographically separated, so that they had to travel every week. Nonetheless, the total succession went very well.

For this president, acting according to his style was a necessity. During the final debriefing in the study's fourth year, he told me that he believed he could not have turned the company around without restructuring it to fit his needs. His successor introduced a series of changes, which again made the organization more product oriented.

RELATIONSHIPS WITH KEY PEOPLE

Perhaps the single most salient difference between the successful and the failed transitions was the quality of the new manager's working relationships at the end of his first year. For example, at this point, three of four managers in the failed successions had poor working relationships with two or more of their key subordinates and with two or more peers, and all had poor working relationships with their superiors. In contrast, in the same time frame, only one of the new administrators in the successful transitions had a poor relationship with his boss and none had poor relationships with two or more people who reported directly to them.

Many reasons were given for these interpersonal problems, such as rivalry issues, disagreement about goals, different beliefs about what constituted effective performance, and conflicts in management style. The underlying common problem, however, was the new managers' failure to develop a set of shared expectations with their key subordinates or their bosses. Without common understanding, each side in the relationships inevitably stopped trusting the other.

The studies showed that developing effective working relationships was a critical task in the taking-hold and immersion stages. If managers didn't explore important differences in the very beginning of their successions, further problems would crop up. Managers in the successful transitions usually confronted problems by the end of the immersion stage and resolved them either by attaining agreement or by parting company.

CONFLICTS IN MANAGEMENT STYLE

Surprisingly, many of the new managers studied (six of 14) described a conflict in styles with their bosses as being a major problem in taking charge. Although conflicts and differences in styles also existed in relationships with subordinates, I am highlighting the problem between new managers and their bosses because this type of discord characterized all but one of the failed successions.

The conflicts always involved control and delegation. In one case, for example, a new general manager five months into the job was exasperated because his boss wouldn't stop a capital request that the manager's predecessor had submitted. The boss had asked his technical and financial staffs to review the situation and was waiting for their report before acting. This manager also reported difficulty in getting quick answers from his boss about operational questions. The manager thought his boss delegated too much and wasn't on top of details.

In contrast, another new executive felt he couldn't get his boss off his back. The situation finally exploded at the end of the first year when his boss gave him a poor performance evaluation for not being involved enough in details and for delegating too much to his subordinates.

In both these cases, the conflicts arose partly because managers hadn't clarified expectations with their bosses but mainly because of less rational factors, including profound beliefs about what is good management. Namely, a good executive sets goals clearly and delegates responsibility to subordinates without interfering, while a good manager gets involved in details and is action oriented and decisive.

How can new managers deal with differences in style? In the cases studied, the new managers had to take the initiative to work out differences and make the accommodations needed for working effectively with their bosses. In the first case, for example, the new manager stopped pressing his boss about the capital project; instead he worked with the two staff groups who were conducting the review. The second manager defined his performance targets specifically with his boss, so the boss could delegate to him more comfortably.

In the three successful transitions marked by sharp style conflicts, the managers employed similar means to deal with them.

HOW STACKED IS THE DECK?

As we can see, many variables influence how well managers take charge. Critical factors range from managers' experience to how effectively they deal with key subordinates and their bosses. Although some are more critical than others, no one factor dominates. Evaluated together, however, they can indicate how much difficulty a new manager will face. Let me illustrate this by returning to the two vignettes that began this article. On the surface they looked so similar, but they turned out so differently.

In the first case, in which the new marketing vice president lasted only nine months, his lack of industry experience hurt him considerably, especially since both his immediate boss and the division's parent management also lacked industry experience. His boss's failure to clarify his expectations about performance and a major conflict in management style between the two men further exacerbated the situation. Finally, a poor working relationship with an important peer, who sought to undermine the new manager, complicated his difficulties.

If the deck is stacked, as it was in this case, unless the new manager or his boss is insightful enough to defuse, compensate for, or in some other way minimize problems, the succession is doomed. In the other case, although the parameters were the same, the dynamics among the players were quite different, so that the second new manager prospered where the other failed.

Managing the New Manager

This study's findings offer several implications that, taken together, challenge a number of assumptions and current practices. First, we can see clearly that understanding a situation and having an impact on it do not occur overnight. Fast-track developmental assignments do not, in the end, benefit the individual, the new unit, or the organization.

Second, the all-purpose general manager who can parachute into any situation and succeed is a myth. Experience and special competencies do matter.

Finally, human variables such as managerial styles make a difference, not only to the organization's climate but also to the business decisions a new manager makes and to how he implements them.

Other soft factors, such as potential conflicts in managerial styles and a newcomer's ability to develop effective working relationships, also seriously affect outcomes. These are, however, subjective factors that often fall into the non-discussable category that senior management seldom considers when it plans successions. Only the savviest planners factor them in and give them the weight they deserve.

Let me be more specific about the findings' implications for both managers who are taking charge and organizations that must be concerned with succession planning and career development.

WHEN YOU ARE TAKING CHARGE

For a manager in the middle of taking charge, this article may be a mixed blessing. On the one hand, it may be a relief to know that the process occurs in stages that consist of predictable learning and action tasks (see the exhibit "Taking Charge: Tasks and Dilemmas" for a summary). On the other, to realize that there may still be considerable learning and action to accomplish after the first three to six months on the job can be a bit dismaying.

The other potentially unsettling implication is that in each of these stages the manager is on a tightrope. For

Taking Charge: Tasks and Dilemmas

	Stage		
I	**Taking hold: orientation and evaluation, corrective actions**	Tasks	Develop an understanding of the new situation
			Take corrective actions
			Develop initial set of priorities and "map" of the situation
			Develop initial set of expectations with key subordinates
			Establish the basis for effective working relationships
		Dilemma	How quickly to act on apparent problems?
			Act too quickly—risks:
			Make a poor decision because of lack of adequate information or knowledge
			Take actions that constrain subsequent decisions that cannot be anticipated yet
			Act too slowly—risks:
			Lose advantages of the "honeymoon" period
			Lose credibility because of apparent indecisiveness
			Lose valuable time
II	**Immersion: fine-grained, exploratory learning and managing the business**	Tasks	Develop a deeper, finer-grained understanding of the new situation and the people
			Assess consequences of taking-hold period actions
			Reassess priorities
			Settle questions and problems concerning key personnel
			Reconfigure "map" of the situation; fill out or revise the concept
			Prepare for reshaping actions

III	**Reshaping: acting on the revised concept**	Tasks	Reconfigure organization based on finer-grained understanding Deal with underlying causes of residual problems Be open to unanticipated problems that emerge as a result of second-wave changes
IV	**Consolidation: evaluative learning, follow-through, and corrective action**	Tasks	Follow through on reshaping actions Deal with unanticipated problems of reshaping stage Remain open to new developments
V	**Refinement: refining operations, looking for new opportunities**		

example, if the taking-hold stage is a bit of a honeymoon, it is also a period in which new managers must establish their credibility. If they act too slowly, they risk losing the honeymoon period's advantages as well as valuable time, and they can appear indecisive. But if new executives act too quickly, they risk making poor decisions because of inadequate knowledge, or they take actions that preclude options they may later wish they had.

Managers who are industry outsiders are on particularly slippery ground. In the absence of good advice or data, they may be better off deferring major changes until they have learned more in the immersion stage. The small first waves of action and large second waves in the outsider successions I studied probably reflect an intuitive recognition of this dilemma.

Finally, interpersonal factors emerge in one fashion or another. If, for example, newcomers find themselves in a managerial style conflict, they should not think it's bizarre; it occurred in almost half the situations I studied.

In general, a comparison of failed and effective transitions indicates that front-end work is crucial, especially in working out parameters and expectations with bosses. In the successful successions, the new managers made their mandates as specific and explicit as possible. They also made a point of keeping their superiors informed, for example, discussing with them changes they were proposing in detail—particularly during the early taking-charge stages. In contrast, the managers who failed carried vague mandates.

The successful managers were also more aware of their limitations in experience or skills and compensated for them either with selective learning or by drawing on their colleagues' abilities.

SUCCESSION PLANNING AND CAREER DEVELOPMENT

As the preceding discussion suggests, top management can take a number of steps to help minimize new administrators' problems. The most obvious of these is making the new person's charter explicit. If this is not possible (because top management doesn't understand the unit's business or the industry is in a period of turmoil), the new manager should know it. For example, in the opening vignette in which the new manager failed after nine months, headquarters hadn't told him that the most urgent priority was to reverse a decline in the newly acquired subsidiary's margins. The innocent new vice president started off buying market share, which inevitably eroded further the margins in the short term.

There are other things companies can do to facilitate the taking-charge process. General Electric, for example, runs assimilation meetings to accelerate working out expectations between new managers and their key subordinates. Conducted by the human resource staff, these meetings give new managers and those who report directly to them the opportunity to talk about expectations and other concerns early in a new manager's tenure. Top management can also anticipate the potential problems new managers who lack relevant experience face, particularly during the taking-charge stages, and lessen them by providing adequate—subordinate or corporate—backup support.

An important implication of this research for succession planning is that taking charge (defined in terms of impact and learning) takes time. Companies that make brief assignments at upper and middle levels will get quick fixes. If assignments are too short for a new manager to go beyond the taking-hold stage, the new manager will deal only with those problems that he or she knows how to fix. That may be enough if a manager's experience base is broad and deep, but when short-term assignments become company policy, both individual units and the organization as a whole suffer eventually. Taken to its extreme, such a policy feeds the obsession with short-term results that many observers have criticized.[2]

Short-term assignments also make little sense from a career development point of view. In most brief assignments, managers can't progress beyond the immersion stage. Yet the payoffs for the organization in substantive change and for the individual in important residual learning and added experience don't come until later. Significant new learning begins in the immersion stage when the outsider is familiar enough to probe underlying issues and subtle cause-and-effect relationships. Managers cannot test this new learning, though, until they act in the reshaping stage, evaluate their actions, and learn more in the consolidation and refinement stages.

The importance of experience also has several implications for succession planning and career development. All other factors being equal, an insider with industry-specific or other relevant experience is more likely to take charge with fewer difficulties than an outsider without industry-specific experience. Three of the four managers who failed were industry outsiders in well-run U.S. and European companies.

The importance of experience, which the study highlighted, also challenges the concept of the professional manager. Although turnaround specialists can succeed in a variety of situations, they are the exception, not the rule; in fact, they are themselves specialists of a kind.

I am not arguing that general management skills don't exist or that people can't transfer them into new settings. I am pointing out that lack of relevant industry or functional experience will make the taking-charge process more difficult, and companies should consider this when planning successions.

When choosing successors to managerial posts, top management has to make some difficult trade-offs in terms of what is good for the person, the unit, and the organization. If one of the organization's objectives is to develop a well-trained pool of managerial talent, then the head office should put executives in assignments that stretch them by broadening their experience. This will inevitably mean putting people with less than optimal experience in charge of units whose performance may suffer, at least in the short term. The question is whether the benefits to the person and to the larger organization are worth the costs. Also, because managers, like all human beings, learn from the feedback of bad as well as good experiences (some may argue they learn more from the ones that turn out badly), top management has to judge how long to keep executives in situations where they are having problems.

On the other hand, if management always assigns people with strong relevant experience, it forfeits giving executives broadening experiences, which become increasingly important at middle and upper levels. The guideline should be to provide developmental assignments that are not totally out of line with a manager's experience and that last long enough to produce important lessons.

Notes

1. John P. Kotter, *The General Managers* (Free Press, 1982).
2. Robert H. Hayes and William J. Abernathy, "Managing Our Way to Economic Decline," HBR July–August 1980.

Originally published in 1985
Reprint R0701k

The Young and the Clueless

KERRY A. BUNKER, KATHY E. KRAM,
AND SHARON TING

Executive Summary

IT'S NATURAL TO PROMOTE your best and brightest, especially when you think they may leave for greener pastures if you don't continually offer them new challenges and rewards. But promoting smart, ambitious young managers too quickly often robs them of the chance to develop the emotional competencies that come with time and experience—competencies like the ability to negotiate with peers, regulate emotions in times of crisis, and win support for change. Indeed, at some point in a manager's career—usually at the vice president level—raw talent and ambition become less important than the ability to influence and persuade, and that's the point at which the emotionally immature manager will lose his effectiveness.

This article argues that delaying a promotion can sometimes be the best thing a senior executive can do for a junior manager. The inexperienced manager who is given time to develop his emotional competencies may be better prepared for the interpersonal demands of top-level leadership. The authors recommend that senior executives employ these strategies to help boost their protégés' people skills: sharpen the 360-degree feedback process, give managers cross-functional assignments to improve their negotiation skills, make the development of emotional competencies mandatory, make emotional competencies a performance measure, and encourage managers to develop informal learning partnerships with peers and mentors.

Delaying a promotion can be difficult given the steadfast ambitions of many junior executives and the hectic pace of organizational life. It may mean going against the norm of promoting people almost exclusively on smarts and business results. It may also mean contending with the disappointment of an esteemed subordinate. But taking the time to build people's emotional competencies isn't an extravagance; it's critical to developing effective leaders.

IN MANY WAYS, 36-year-old Charles Armstrong is a natural leader. He's brilliant, creative, energetic, aggressive—a strategic and financial genius. He's risen quickly through the ranks due to his keen business instincts and proven ability to deliver bottom-line results, at times jumping from one organization to another to leapfrog through the hierarchy. But now his current job is on the line. A division president at an international consumer products company, he's just uncovered a major production setback on a heavily promoted new product. Thousands of orders have been delayed, customers are furious, and the company's stock price has plummeted since the news went public.

Worse, the crisis was utterly preventable. Had Armstrong understood the value of building relationships with his peers and had his subordinates found him approachable, he might have been able to appreciate the cross-functional challenges of developing this particular product. He might have learned of the potential delay months earlier instead of at the eleventh hour. He could have postponed a national advertising campaign and set expectations with investors. He might have even found a way to solve the problems and launch the product on time. But despite his ability to dazzle his superiors with talent and intellect, Armstrong is widely viewed by his peers and subordinates as self-promoting, intolerant, and remote. Perhaps worse, he's only half aware of how others perceive him, and to the extent he does know, he's not terribly concerned. These relationships are not a priority for him. Like so many other talented young managers, Armstrong lacks the emotional competencies that would enable him to work more effectively as part of a team. And now his bosses seem to have unwittingly undermined his career, having promoted him too quickly, before he could develop the relationship skills he needs.

Break the Pattern

What happened with Charles Armstrong is an increasingly common phenomenon. In the past ten years, we've met dozens of managers who have fallen victim to a harmful mix of their own ambition and their bosses' willingness to overlook a lack of people skills. (As with all the examples in these pages, we've changed Armstrong's name and other identifying features to protect our clients' identities.) Indeed, most executives seek out smart, aggressive people, paying more attention to their accomplishments than to their emotional maturity. What's more, they know that their strongest performers have options—if they don't get the job they want at one company, they're bound to get it somewhere else. Why risk losing them to a competitor by delaying a promotion?

The answer is that promoting them can be just as risky. Putting these unseasoned managers into positions of authority too quickly robs them of the opportunity to develop the emotional competencies that come with time and experience—competencies like the ability to negotiate with peers, regulate their emotions in times of crisis, or win support for change. Bosses may be delighted with such managers' intelligence and passion—and may even see younger versions of themselves—but peers and subordinates are more likely to see them as arrogant and inconsiderate, or, at the very least, aloof. And therein lies the problem. At some point in a young manager's career, usually at the vice president level, raw talent and determined ambition become less important than the ability to influence and persuade. And unless senior executives appreciate this fact and make emotional competence a top priority, these high-potential managers will continue to fail, often at significant cost to the company.

Research has shown that the higher a manager rises in the ranks, the more important soft leadership skills are to his success.[1] Our colleagues at the Center for Creative Leadership have found that about a third of senior executives derail or plateau at some point, most often due to an emotional deficit such as the inability to build a team or regulate their own emotions in times of stress. And in our combined 55 years of coaching and teaching, we've seen firsthand how a young manager risks his career when he fails to develop emotional competencies. But the problem isn't youth per se. The problem is a lack of emotional maturity, which doesn't come easily or automatically and isn't something you learn from a book. It's one thing to understand the importance of relationships at an intellectual level and to learn techniques like active listening; it's another matter entirely to develop a full range of interpersonal competencies like patience, openness, and empathy. Emotional maturity involves a fundamental shift in self-awareness and behavior, and that change requires practice, diligence, and time.

Armstrong's boss admits that he may have promoted the young manager too soon: "I was just like Charles when I was his age, but I was a director, not a division president. It's easier to make mistakes and learn when you aren't in such a big chair. I want him to succeed, and I think he could make a great CEO one day, but sometimes he puts me at risk. He's just too sure of himself to listen." And so, in many cases, executives do their employees and the company a service by delaying the promotion of a young manager and giving him the chance to develop his interpersonal skills. Interrupting the manager's ascent long enough to round out his experience will usually yield a much more effective and stable leader.

This article will look at five strategies for boosting emotional competencies and redirecting managers who are paying a price for damaged or nonexistent relationships. The strategies aren't terribly complicated, but implementing them and getting people to change their entrenched behaviors can be very difficult. Many of these managers are accustomed to receiving accolades, and it often isn't easy for them to hear—or act on—difficult messages. You may have to satisfy yourself with small victories and accept occasional slipups. But perhaps the greatest challenge is having the discipline to resist the charm of the young and the clueless—to refrain from promoting them before they are ready and to stay the course even if they threaten to quit.

Deepen 360-Degree Feedback

With its questionnaires and standardized rating scales, 360-degree feedback as it is traditionally implemented may not be sufficiently specific or detailed to get the attention of inexperienced managers who excel at bottom-line measures but struggle with more subtle relationship challenges. These managers will benefit from a deeper and more thorough process that includes time for reflection and follow-up conversations. That means, for example, interviewing a wider range of the manager's peers and subordinates and giving her the opportunity to read verbatim responses to open-ended questions. Such detailed and extensive feedback can help a person see herself more as others do, a must for the young manager lacking the self-awareness to understand where she's falling short.

We witnessed this lack of self-awareness in Bill Miller, a 42-year-old vice president at a software company—an environment where technical ability is highly prized. Miller had gone far on pure intellect, but he never fully appreciated his own strengths. So year after year, in assignment after assignment, he worked doubly hard at learning the complexities of the business, neglecting his relationships with his colleagues as an unintended consequence. His coworkers considered his smarts and business acumen among the finest in the company, but they found him unapproachable and detached. As a result, top management questioned his ability to lead the type of strategic change that would require motivating staff at all levels. Not until Miller went through an in-depth 360-degree developmental review was he able to accept that he no longer needed to prove his intelligence—that he could relax in that respect and instead work on strengthening his personal connections. After months of working hard to cultivate stronger relationships with his employees, Miller began to notice that he felt more included in chance social encounters like hallway conversations.

Art Grainger, a 35-year-old senior manager at a cement and concrete company, was generally considered a champion by his direct reports. He was also known for becoming defensive whenever his peers or superiors questioned or even discussed his unit's performance. Through 360-degree reviews, he discovered that while everyone saw him as committed, results-oriented, and technically brilliant, they also saw him as overly protective, claiming he resisted any action or decision that might affect his department. Even his employees felt that he kept them isolated from the rest of the company, having said he reviewed all memos between departments, didn't invite people from other parts of the company to his department's meetings, and openly criticized other managers. Only when Grainger heard that his staff agreed with what his bosses had been telling him for years did he concede that he needed to change. Since then, he has come to see members of other departments as potential allies and has tried to redefine his team to include people from across the company.

It's worth noting that many of these smart young managers aren't used to hearing criticism. Consequently, they may discount negative feedback, either because the comments don't mesh with what they've heard in previous conversations or because their egos are so strong. Or they may conclude that they can "fix" the problem right away—after all, they've been able to fix most problems they've encountered in the past. But developing emotional competencies requires practice and ongoing personal interactions. The good news is that if you succeed in convincing them that these issues are career threatening, they may apply the same zeal to their emotional development that they bring to their other projects. And that's why 360-degree feedback is so valuable: When it comes from multiple sources and is ongoing, it's difficult to ignore.

Interrupt the Ascent

When people are continually promoted within their areas of expertise, they don't have to stray far from their comfort zones, so they seldom need to ask for help, especially if they're good problem solvers. Accordingly, they may become overly independent and fail to cultivate relationships with people who could be useful to them in the future. What's more, they may rely on the authority that comes with rank rather than learning how to influence people. A command-and-control mentality may work in certain situations, particularly in lower to middle management, but it's usually insufficient in more senior positions, when peer relationships are critical and success depends more on the ability to move hearts and minds than on the ability to develop business solutions.

We sometimes counsel our clients to broaden young managers' skills by assigning them to cross-functional roles outside their expected career paths. This is distinct from traditional job rotation, which has employees spending time in different functional areas to enhance and broaden their knowledge of the business. Rather, the manager is assigned a role in which he doesn't have much direct authority. This will help him focus on developing other skills like negotiation and influencing peers.

Consider the case of Sheila McIntyre, a regional sales director at a technology company. McIntyre had been promoted quickly into the managerial ranks because she consistently outsold her colleagues month after month. In her early thirties, she began angling for another promotion—this time, to vice president—but her boss, Ron Meyer, didn't think she was ready. Meyer felt that McIntyre had a quick temper and little patience for people whom she perceived as less visionary. So he put the promotion on hold, despite McIntyre's stellar performance, and created a yearlong special assignment for her—heading a team investigating cross-selling opportunities. To persuade her to take the job, he not only explained that it would help McIntyre broaden her skills but promised a significant financial reward if she succeeded, also hinting that the hoped-for promotion would follow. It was a stretch for McIntyre. She had to use her underdeveloped powers of persuasion to win support from managers in other divisions. But in the end, her team presented a brilliant cross-selling strategy, which the company implemented over the following year. More important, she developed solid relationships with a number of influential people throughout the organization and learned a lot about the value of others' insights and experiences. McIntyre was eventually promoted to vice president, and to Meyer's satisfaction, her new reports now see her not just as a super-star salesperson but as a well-connected manager who can negotiate on their behalf.

Such cross-functional assignments—with no clear authority or obvious ties to a career path—can be a tough sell. It's not easy to convince young managers that these assignments are valuable, nor is it easy to help them extract relevant knowledge. If the managers feel marginalized, they may not stick around. Remember Bill Miller, the vice president who had neglected his emotional skills in his zeal to learn the business? While he was successful in some of his early informal attempts to build relationships, he was confused and demoralized when his boss, Jerry Schulman, gave him a special assignment to lead a task force reviewing internal processes. Miller had expected a promotion, and the new job didn't feel "real." Schulman made the mistake of not telling Miller that he saw the job as an ideal networking opportunity, so Miller began to question his future at the company. A few months into the new job, Miller gave his notice. He seized an opportunity—a step up—at an archrival, taking a tremendous amount of talent and institutional knowledge with him. Had Schulman shared his reasoning with Miller, he might have retained one of his most valuable players—one who had already seen the importance of developing his emotional competence and had begun to make progress.

Act On Your Commitment

One of the reasons employees get stuck in the pattern we've described is that their bosses point out deficits in emotional competencies but don't follow through. They either neglect to articulate the consequences of continuing the destructive behavior or make empty threats but proceed with a promotion anyway. The hard-charging young executive can only conclude that these competencies are optional.

A cautionary tale comes from Mitchell Geller who, at 29, was on the verge of being named partner at a law firm. He had alienated many of his peers and subordinates over the years through his arrogance, a shortcoming duly noted on his yearly performance reviews, yet his keen legal mind had won him promotion after promotion. With Geller's review approaching, his boss, Larry Snow, pointed to heavy attrition among the up-and-coming lawyers who worked for Geller and warned him that further advancement would be contingent on a change in personal style. Geller didn't take the feedback to heart—he was confident that he'd get by, as he always had, on sheer talent. And true to form, Snow didn't stick to his guns. The promotion came through even though Geller's behavior hadn't changed. Two weeks later, Geller, by then a partner responsible for managing client relationships, led meetings with two key accounts. Afterward, the first client approached Snow and asked him to sit in on future meetings. Then the second client withdrew his business altogether, complaining that Geller had refused to listen to alternative points of view.

Contrast Geller's experience with that of 39-year-old Barry Kessler, a senior vice president at an insurance company. For years, Kessler had been heir apparent to the CEO due to his strong financial skills and vast knowledge of the business—that is, until John Mason, his boss and the current CEO, began to question the wisdom of promoting him.

While Kessler managed his own group exceptionally well, he avoided collaboration with other units, which was particularly important as the company began looking for new growth opportunities, including potential alliances with other organizations. The problem wasn't that Kessler was hostile, it was that he was passively disengaged—a flaw that hadn't seemed as important when he was responsible only for his own group. In coaching Kessler, we learned that he was extremely averse to conflict and that he avoided situations where he couldn't be the decision maker. His aversions sharply limited his ability to work with peers.

Mason sent a strong signal, not only to Kessler but to others in the organization, when he essentially demoted Kessler by taking away some of his responsibilities and temporarily pulling him from the succession plan. To give Kessler an opportunity to develop the skills he lacked, Mason asked him to lead a cross-functional team dedicated to finding strategic opportunities for growth. Success would require Kessler to devote more time to developing his interpersonal skills. He had no authority over the other team members, so he had to work through disputes and help the team arrive at a consensus. Two years later, Kessler reports that he is more comfortable with conflict and feedback, and he's worked his way back into the succession plan.

By the way, it's counterproductive to hold managers to a certain standard of behavior without showing that the same standard applies to everyone, right up to top management. In many cases, that means acknowledging your own development goals, which isn't easy. One CEO we worked with, Joe Simons, came to realize during 360-degree feedback and peer coaching that his personal style was interfering with his subordinates' growth.

Simons had declared innovation a corporate priority, yet his fear of failure led him to micromanage his employees, stifling their creativity. To stop this pattern and express his new-found commitment to improving his relationship skills, he revealed his personal goals—to seek advice more regularly and to communicate more openly—to his direct reports. He promised to change specific behaviors and asked for the team's feedback and support in this process. Going public with these goals was tough for Simons, a private person raised on traditional command-and-control leadership. Admitting that he needed to change some behaviors felt dangerously weak to him, especially given that the company was going through a difficult time and employees were looking to him for assurance, but his actions made his new priorities clear to employees.

Simons's candor won people's trust and respect, and over the course of many months, others in the company began to reflect more openly on their own emotional skills and engage in similar processes of personal development. Not only did his relationships with his direct reports improve, but Simons became a catalyst and model for others as well. He told us of an encounter with Gwen Marshall, the company's CFO and one of Simons's direct reports. Marshall was concerned about a new hire who wasn't coming up to speed as quickly as she had hoped—he was asking lots of questions and, she felt, not taking enough initiative. She had just snapped at him at the close of a meeting, and he'd looked surprised and angry. In speaking to Simons about the incident, however, she acknowledged that her impatience was perhaps unfair. He was, after all, new to the job. What's more, the nature of finance demanded precise thinking and a thorough knowledge of the business. Marshall ended the conversation by saying she would apologize to the new employee. Simons was surprised at Marshall's comments—he was used to seeing her simply blow off steam and move on to the next task. But possibly due to Simons's example, she had become more attuned to the importance of her own emotional competence. Such reflection has become a habit among Simons's team—a change that has enhanced personal relationships and increased the team's overall performance.

Institutionalize Personal Development

One of the most effective ways to build managers' emotional competencies is to weave interpersonal goals into the fabric of the organization, where everyone is expected to demonstrate a specific set of emotional skills and where criteria for promotion include behaviors as well as technical ability. A built-in process will make it easier to uncover potential problems early and reduce the chances that people identified as needing personal development will feel singled out or unfairly held back. Employees will know exactly what's expected of them and what it takes to advance in their careers.

Here's a case in which institutionalizing personal development was extremely effective: Mark Jones is an executive who was tapped for the CEO job at a major manufacturing company on the condition that he engage a coach because of his reputation for being too blunt and aggressive. A yearlong coaching relationship helped Jones understand the pitfalls associated with his style, and he decided that others could benefit from arriving at such an understanding far earlier in their careers. To that end, he launched several major initiatives to shape the company culture in such a way that personal and professional learning were not only encouraged but expected.

First, he articulated a new set of corporate values and practices that were based on meeting business objectives and developing top-notch leadership skills. One of the values was "Dare to be transparent," which meant that all employees, especially those in senior leadership roles, were expected to be open about their weaknesses, ask for help, and offer honest, constructive feedback to their peers. Knowing that it would be necessary to create incentives and rewards for these new behaviors, Jones took an active role in the review and personal-development goals of the company's top 100 executives, and he mandated that all employees' performance plans incorporate specific actions related to developing their own emotional competencies. Jones also made emotional skills a key qualification in the search for a successor—a requirement that many organizations pay lip service to. Many of them often overvalue raw intellect and depth of knowledge, largely because of the war for talent, which has resulted in a singular focus on hiring and retaining the best and brightest regardless of their emotional competence. Finally, Jones created a new position, corporate learning officer; he and the CLO partnered with a nearby university to create a learning institute where corporate executives could teach in and attend leadership programs. Jones himself is a frequent lecturer and participant in the various courses.

Through all these actions, Jones has made it clear that employees need to make continual learning and emotional development a priority. He's also emphasized that everyone from the CEO on down is expected to set goals for improving personal skills. Since implementing the program, he is finding it easier to attract and retain talented young executives—indeed, his organization has evolved from a recruiter's nightmare to a magnet for young talent. It is becoming known as a place where emerging leaders can find real opportunities to learn and grow.

We worked with another company where the senior management team committed to developing the emotional competencies of the company's leaders. The team first provided extensive education on coaching to the HR department, which in turn supervised a program whereby top managers coached their younger and more inexperienced colleagues. The goal was to have both the experienced and inexperienced benefit: The junior managers provided feedback on the senior people's coaching skills, and the senior people helped foster emotional competencies in their less-experienced colleagues.

The results were encouraging. Wes Burke, an otherwise high-performing manager, had recently been struggling to meet his business targets. After spending time with Burke and conferring with his subordinates and peers, his coach (internal to the organization) came to believe that, in his zest to achieve his goals, Burke was unable to slow down and listen to other people's ideas. Burke wasn't a boor: He had taken courses in communication and knew how to fake listening behaviors such as nodding his head and giving verbal acknowledgments, but he was often distracted and not really paying attention. He never accepted this feedback until one day, while he was walking purposefully through the large operations plant he managed, a floor supervisor stopped him to discuss his ideas for solving an ongoing production problem. Burke flipped on his active-listening mode. After uttering a few acknowledgments and saying, "Thanks, let's talk more about that," he moved on, leaving the supervisor feeling frustrated and at a loss for how to capture his boss's interest. As it happened, Burke's coach was watching. He pulled the young manager aside and said, "You didn't hear a word Karl just said. You weren't really listening." Burke admitted as much to himself and his coach. He then apologized to Karl, much to the supervisor's surprise. Keeping this incident in mind helped Burke remember the importance of his working relationships. His coach had also helped him realize that he shouldn't have assumed his sheer will and drive would somehow motivate his employees. Burke had been wearing people down, physically and psychologically. A year later, Burke's operation was hitting its targets, an accomplishment he partially attributes to the one-on-one coaching he received.

Cultivate Informal Networks

While institutionalized programs to build emotional competencies are critical, some managers will benefit more from an informal network of relationships that fall outside the company hierarchy. Mentoring, for example, can help both junior and senior managers further their emotional development through a new type of relationship. And when the mentoring experience is a positive one, it often acts as a springboard to a rich variety of relationships with others throughout the organization. In particular, it gives junior managers a chance to experience different leadership styles and exposes them to diverse viewpoints.

Sonia Greene, a 32-year-old manager at a consulting firm, was hoping to be promoted to principal, but she hadn't raised the issue with her boss because she assumed he didn't think she was ready, and she didn't want to create tension. She was a talented consultant with strong client relationships, but her internal relationships were weak due to a combination of shyness, an independent nature, and a distaste for conflict, which inhibited her from asking for feedback. When her company launched a mentoring program, Greene signed up, and through a series of lengthy conversations with Jessica Burnham, a partner at the firm, she developed new insights about her strengths and weaknesses. The support of an established player such as Burnham helped Greene become more confident and honest in her development discussions with her boss, who hadn't been aware that Greene was willing to receive and act on feedback. Today, Greene is armed with a precise understanding of what she needs to work on and is well on her way to being promoted. What's more, her relationship with Burnham has prompted her to seek out other connections, including a peer group of up-and-coming managers who meet monthly to share experiences and offer advice to one another.

Peer networking is beneficial to even the most top-level executives. And the relationships needn't be confined within organizational boundaries. Joe Simons, a CEO we mentioned earlier, wanted to continue his own personal development, so he cultivated a relationship with another executive he'd met through our program. The two men have stayed in touch through regular e-mails and phone calls, keeping their discussions confidential so they can feel free to share even the most private concerns. They also get together periodically to discuss their goals for personal development. Both have found these meetings invaluable, noting that their work relationships have continued to improve and that having a trustworthy confidant has helped each avoid relapsing into old habits during times of stress.

Delaying a promotion can be difficult given the steadfast ambitions of the young executive and the hectic pace of organizational life, which makes personal learning seem like an extravagance. It requires a delicate balance of honesty and support, of patience and goading. It means going against the norm of promoting people almost exclusively on smarts, talent, and business results. It also means contending with the disappointment of an esteemed subordinate.

But taking the time to build people's emotional competencies isn't an extravagance; it's critical to developing effective leaders. Give in to the temptation to promote your finest before they're ready, and you're left with executives who may thrive on change and demonstrate excellent coping and survival skills but who lack the self-awareness, empathy, and social abilities required to foster and nurture those strengths in others. MBA programs and management books can't teach young executives everything they need to know about people skills. Indeed, there's no substitute for experience, reflection, feedback, and, above all, practice.

Think Before Promoting

IT'S NOT UNUSUAL for a star performer to be promoted into higher management before he's ready. Yes, he may be exceptionally smart and talented, but he may also lack essential people skills. Rather than denying him the promotion altogether, his boss might do well to delay it—and use that time to help develop the candidate's emotional competencies. Here's how.

Deepen 360-Degree Feedback

Go beyond the usual set of questionnaires that make up the traditional 360-degree-feedback process. Interview a wide variety of the manager's peers and subordinates and let him read verbatim responses to open-ended performance questions.

Interrupt the Ascent

Help the inexperienced manager get beyond a command-and-control mentality by pushing him to develop his negotiation and persuasion skills. Instead of promoting him, give him cross-functional assignments where he can't rely on rank to influence people.

Act On Your Commitment

Don't give the inexperienced manager the impression that emotional competencies are optional. Hold him accountable for his interpersonal skills, in some cases taking a tough stance by demoting him or denying him a promotion, but with the promise that changed behaviors will ultimately be rewarded.

Institutionalize Personal Development

Weave interpersonal goals into the fabric of the organization and make emotional competence a performance measure. Also work to institute formal development programs that teach leadership skills and facilitate self-awareness, reflection, and opportunities to practice new emotional competencies.

Cultivate Informal Networks

Encourage the manager to develop informal learning partnerships with peers and mentors in order to expose him to different leadership styles and perspectives. This will provide him with honest and ongoing feedback and continual opportunities to learn.

Note

1. In his HBR articles "What Makes a Leader?" (November–December 1998) and "Primal Leadership: The Hidden Driver of Great Performance" (with Richard Boyatzis and Annie McKee, December 2001), Daniel Goleman makes the case that emotional competence is the crucial driver of a leader's success.

Originally published in December 2002
Reprint R0212F

Saving Your Rookie Managers from Themselves

CAROL A. WALKER

Executive Summary

MOST ORGANIZATIONS PROMOTE employees into managerial positions based on their technical competence. But very often, that kind of competence does not translate into good managerial performance. Many rookie managers fail to grasp how their roies have changed: that their jobs are no longer about personal achievement but about enabling others to achieve, that sometimes driving the bus means taking a backseat, and that building a team is often more important than cutting a deal. Even the best employees have trouble adjusting to these new realties, and that trouble can be exacerbated by the normal insecurities that may make rookie managers hesitant to ask for help.

The dynamic unfolds something like this: As rookie managers internalize their stress, their focus, too, becomes increasingly internal. They become insecure and self-focused and cannot properly support their teams. Invariably, trust breaks down, staff members become alienated, and productivity suffers.

In this article, coach and management consultant Carol Walker, who works primarily with rookie managers and their supervisors, addresses the five problem areas that rookie managers typically face: delegating, getting support from senior staffers, projecting confidence, thinking strategically, and giving feedback. You may think these elements sound like Management 101, and you'd be right, Walker writes. But these basic elements are also what trip up most managers in the early stages of their careers (and even, she admits, throughout their careers). The bosses of rookie managers have a responsibility to anticipate and address these problems; not doing so will hurt the rookie, the boss, and the company overall.

TOM EDELMAN, LIKE A MILLION freshly minted managers before him, had done a marvelous job as an individual contributor. He was smart, confident, forward thinking, and resourceful. His clients liked him, as did his boss and coworkers. Consequently, no one in the department was surprised when his boss offered him a managerial position. Tom accepted with some ambivalence—he loved working directly with clients and was loath to give that up—but on balance, he was thrilled.

Six months later, when I was called into coach Tom (I've disguised his name), I had trouble even picturing the confident insider he once had been. He looked like a deer caught in the headlights. Tom seemed overwhelmed and indeed even used that word several times to describe how he felt. He had started to doubt his abilities. His direct reports, once close colleagues, no longer seemed to respect or even like him. What's more, his department had been beset by a series of small crises, and Tom spent most of his time putting out these fires. He knew this wasn't the most effective use of his time, but he didn't know how to stop. These problems hadn't yet translated into poor business results, but he was in trouble nonetheless.

His boss realized that he was in danger of failing and brought me in to assist. With support and coaching, Tom got the help he needed and eventually became an effective manager. Indeed, he has been promoted twice since I worked with him, and he now runs a small division within the same company. But his near failure—and the path that brought him to that point—is surprisingly typical. Most organizations promote employees into managerial positions based on their technical competence. Very often, however, those people fail to grasp how their roles have changed—that their jobs are no longer about personal achievement but instead about enabling others to achieve, that sometimes driving the bus means taking a backseat, and that building a team is often more important than cutting a deal. Even the best employees can have trouble adjusting to these new realities. That trouble may be exacerbated by normal insecurities that make rookie managers hesitant to ask for help, even when they find themselves in thoroughly unfamiliar territory. As these new managers internalize their stress, their focus becomes internal as well. They become insecure and self-focused and cannot properly support their teams. Inevitably, trust breaks down, staff members are alienated, and productivity suffers.

Many companies unwittingly support this downward spiral by assuming that their rookie managers will somehow learn critical management skills by osmosis. Some rookies do, to be sure, but in my experience they're the exceptions. Most need more help. In the absence of comprehensive training and intensive coaching—which most companies don't offer—the rookie manager's boss plays a key role. Of course, it's not possible for most senior managers to spend hours and hours every week overseeing a new manager's work, but if you know what typical challenges a rookie manager faces, you'll be able to anticipate some problems before they arise and nip others in the bud.

Delegating

Effective delegation may be one of the most difficult tasks for rookie managers. Senior managers bestow on them big responsibilities and tight deadlines, and they put a lot of pressure on them to produce results. The natural response of rookies when faced with such challenges is to "just do it," thinking that's what got them promoted in the first place. But their reluctance to delegate assignments also has its roots in some very real fears. First is the fear of losing stature: If I assign high-profile projects to my staff members, they'll get the credit. What kind of visibility will I be left with? Will it be clear to my boss and my staff what value I'm adding? Second is the fear of abdicating control: If I allow Frank to do this, how can I be sure that he will do it correctly?

In the face of this fear, the rookie manager may delegate tasks but supervise Frank so closely that he will never feel accountable. Finally, the rookie may be hesitant to delegate work because he's afraid of overburdening his staff. He may be uncomfortable assigning work to former peers for fear that they'll resent him. But the real resentment usually comes when staff members feel that lack of opportunity is blocking their advancement.

Signs that these fears may be playing out include new managers who work excessively long hours, are hesitant to take on new responsibilities, have staff members who seem unengaged, or have a tendency to answer on behalf of employees instead of encouraging them to communicate with you directly.

The first step toward helping young managers delegate effectively is to get them to understand their new role. Acknowledge that their job fundamentally differs from an individual contributor's. Clarify what you and the organization value in leaders. Developing talented, promotable staff is critical in any company. Let new managers know that they will be rewarded for these less tangible efforts in addition to hitting numerical goals. Understanding this new role is half the battle for rookie managers, and one that many companies mistakenly assume is evident from the start.

After clarifying how your rookie manager's role has changed, you can move on to tactics. Perhaps it goes without saying, but you should lead by example. You have the responsibility to empower the rookie who works for you and do what you can to help him overcome his insecurities about his value to the organization. You can then assist him in looking for opportunities to empower and engage his team.

One young manager I worked with desperately needed to find time to train and supervise new employees. His firm had been recently acquired, and he had to deal with high staff turnover and new industrywide rules and regulations. The most senior person on his staff—a woman who had worked for the acquiring company—was about to return from an extended family leave, and he was convinced that he couldn't ask her for help. After all, she had a part-time schedule, and she'd asked to be assigned to the company's largest client. To complicate matters, he suspected that she resented his promotion. As we evaluated the situation, the manager was able to see that the senior staffer's number one priority was reestablishing herself as an important part of the team. Once he realized this, he asked her to take on critical supervisory responsibilities, balanced with a smaller client load, and she eagerly agreed. Indeed, she returned from leave excited about partnering with her manager to develop the team.

When a new manager grumbles about mounting workloads, seize the opportunity to discuss delegation. Encourage him to take small risks initially, playing to the obvious strengths of his staff members. Asking his super-organized, reliable assistant to take the lead in handling the logistics of a new product launch, for example, is much less risky than asking a star salesperson, unaccustomed to this sort of detailed work, to do it. Early successes will build the manager's confidence and willingness to take progressively larger risks in stretching each team member's capabilities. Reinforce to him that delegation does not mean abdication. Breaking a complex project into manageable chunks, each with clearly defined milestones, makes effective follow-up easier. It's also important to schedule regular meetings before the project even begins in order to ensure that the manager stays abreast of progress and that staff members feel accountable.

Getting Support from Above

Most first-time managers see their relationship with their boss more as one of servitude than of partnership. They will wait for you to initiate meetings, ask for reports, and question results. You may welcome this restraint, but generally it's a bad sign. For one thing, it puts undue pressure on you to keep the flow of communication going. Even more important, it prevents new managers from looking to you as a critical source of support. If they don't see you that way, it's unlikely that they will see themselves that way for their own people. The problem isn't only that your position intimidates them; it's also that they fear being vulnerable. A newly promoted manager doesn't want you to see weaknesses, lest you think you made a mistake in promoting her. When I ask rookie managers about their relationships with their bosses, they often admit that they are trying to "stay under the boss's radar" and are "careful about what [they] say to the boss."

Some inexperienced managers will not seek your help even when they start to founder. Seemingly capable rookie managers often try to cover up a failing project or relationship—just until they can get it back under control. For example, one manager I worked with at a technology company hired a professional 20 years her senior. The transition was rocky, and, despite her best efforts, the individual wasn't acclimating to the organization. (The company, like many in the technology sector, was very youth oriented.) Rather than reaching out to her boss for help, the manager continued to grapple with the situation alone. The staff member ultimately resigned at the busiest time of the year, and the young manager suffered the dual punishment of being understaffed at the worst possible moment and having it known that she had lost a potentially important contributor.

What's the boss of a rookie manager to do? You can begin by clarifying expectations. Explain the connection between the rookie's success and your success, so that she understands that open communication is necessary for you to achieve your goals. Explain that you don't expect her to have all the answers. Introduce her to other managers within the company who may be helpful, and encourage her to contact them as needed. Let her know that mistakes happen but that the cover-up is always worse than the crime. Let her know that you like to receive occasional lunch invitations as much as you like to extend them.

Lunch and drop-by meetings are important, but they usually aren't enough. Consider meeting regularly with a new manager—perhaps weekly in the early stages of a new assignment, moving to biweekly or monthly as her confidence builds. These meetings will develop rapport, provide you with insight into how the person is approaching the job, and make the new manager organize her thoughts on a regular basis. Be clear that the meetings are her time and that it's up to her to plan the agenda.You're there to ask and answer questions and to offer advice. The message you send is that the individual's work is important to you and that you're a committed business partner. More subtly, you're modeling how to simultaneously empower and guide direct reports.

Projecting Confidence

Looking confident when you don't feel confident—it's a challenge we all face, and as senior managers we're usually conscious of the need when it arises. Rookie managers are often so internally focused that they are unaware of this need or the image they project. They are so focused on substance that they forget that form counts, too. The first weeks and months on the job are a critical time for new leaders to reach out to staff. If they don't project confidence, they are unlikely to inspire and energize their teams.

I routinely work with new managers who are unaware that their everyday demeanor is hurting their organizations. In one rapidly growing technology company, the service manager, Linda, faced high levels of stress. Service outages were all too common, and they were beyond her control. Customers were exacting, and they too were under great pressure. Her rapidly growing staff was generally inexperienced. Distraught customers and employees had her tied up in knots almost daily. She consistently appeared breathless, rushed, and fearful that the other shoe was about to drop. The challenge was perhaps too big for a first-time manager, but that's what happens in rapidly growing companies. On one level, Linda was doing an excellent job keeping the operation going. The client base was growing and retention was certainly high—largely as a result of her energy and resourcefulness. But on another level, she was doing a lot of damage.

Linda's frantic demeanor had two critical repercussions. First, she had unwittingly defined the standard for acceptable conduct in her department, and her inexperienced staff began to display the same behaviors. Before long, other departments were reluctant to communicate with Linda or her team, for fear of bothering them or eliciting an emotional reaction. But for the company to arrive at real solutions to the service problems, departments needed to openly exchange information, and that wasn't happening. Second, Linda was not portraying herself to senior managers as promotion material. They were pleased with her troubleshooting abilities, but they did not see a confident, thoughtful senior manager in the making. The image Linda was projecting would ultimately hold back both her career and her department.

Not all rookie managers display the problems that Linda did. Some appear excessively arrogant. Others wear their self-doubt on their sleeves. Whether your managers appear overwhelmed, arrogant, or insecure, honest feedback is your best tool. You can help rookie managers by telling them that it's always safe to let out their feelings—in your office, behind closed doors. Reinforce just how long a shadow they cast once they assume leadership positions. Their staff members watch them closely, and if they see professionalism and optimism, they are likely to demonstrate those characteristics as well. Preach the gospel of conscious comportment—a constant awareness of the image one is projecting to the world. If you observe a manager projecting a less-than-positive image, tell that person right away.

You should also be alert to new managers who undermine their own authority. Linda made another classic rookie mistake when she attempted to get her staff members to implement an initiative that her boss had come up with. In presenting the initiative, she let her team know it was important to implement because it had come from the division's senior vice president. While her intentions were good—rallying the team to perform—her words encouraged the group to focus attention above her rather than on her. There is no quicker way for a rookie manager to lose credibility with her staff than to appear to be a mouthpiece for senior management. Pointing out that senior management will be checking up on the initiative certainly won't hurt, but the rookie manager must take care never to be perceived simply as the messenger.

Just-in-time coaching is often the most effective method for showing rookie managers how to project confidence. For instance, the first time you ask a new manager to carry out an initiative, take a little extra time to walk her through the process. Impress upon her the cardinal rule of management: Your staff members don't necessarily have to like you, but they do need to trust you. Ensure that the new manager owns the message she's delivering.

Layoffs are a classic example of a message the rookie manager will struggle with. Don't allow a rookie to proceed half-prepared. Share as much information as you can. Make sure she's ready for all the likely questions and reactions by asking her to do an informal dry run with you. You might be surprised by how poorly she conveys the message in her first few attempts. A little practice may preserve the image of your manager and your company.

Focusing on the Big Picture

Rookie managers have a real knack for allowing immediate tasks to overshadow overarching initiatives. This is particularly true for those promoted from within, because they've just come from the front lines where they're accustomed to constant fire fighting. As a recent individual contributor armed with plenty of technical know-how, the rookie manager instinctively runs to the immediate rescue of any client or staff member in need. The sense of accomplishment rookies get from such rescues is seductive and far more exhilarating than rooting out the cause of all the fire fighting. And what could be better for team spirit than having the boss jump into the trenches and fight the good fight?

Of course, a leader shows great team spirit if he joins the troops in emergencies. But are all those emergencies true emergencies? Are newer staff members being empowered to handle complex challenges? And if the rookie manager is busy fighting fires, who is thinking strategically for the department? If you're the senior manager and these questions are popping into your head, you may well have a rookie manager who doesn't fully understand his role or is afraid to seize it.

I recently worked with a young manager who had become so accustomed to responding to a steady flow of problems that he was reluctant to block off any time to work on the strategic initiatives we had identified. When I probed, he revealed that he felt a critical part of his role was to wait for crises to arise."What if I schedule this time and something urgent comes up and I disappoint someone?"he asked. When I pointed out that he could always postpone his strategy sessions if a true emergency arose, he seemed relieved. But he saw the concept of making time to think about the business as self-indulgent—this, despite the fact that his group was going to be asked to raise productivity significantly in the following fiscal year, and he'd done nothing to prepare for that reality.

Senior managers can help rookies by explaining to them that strategic thinking is a necessary skill for career advancement: For first-time managers, 10% of the work might be strategic and 90% tactical. As executives climb the corporate ladder, however, those percentages will flip-flop. To be successful at the next level, managers must demonstrate that they can think and act strategically. You can use your regularly scheduled meetings to help your managers focus on the big picture. Don't allow them to simply review the latest results and move on. Ask probing questions about those results. For example,"What trends are you seeing in the marketplace that could affect you in two quarters? Tell me how your competition is responding to those same trends." Don't let them regale you with the wonderful training their staffs have been getting without asking, "What additional skills do we need to build in the staff to increase productivity by 25% next year?" If you aren't satisfied with your managers' responses, let them know that you expect them to think this way—not to have all the answers, but to be fully engaged in the strategic thought process.

Rookie managers commonly focus on activities rather than on goals. That's because activities can be accomplished quickly (for example, conducting a seminar to improve the sales staff's presentation skills), whereas achieving goals generally takes more time (for example, actually enhancing the sales staff's effectiveness). The senior manager can help the rookie manager think strategically by asking for written goals that clearly distinguish between the goals and their supporting activities. Insisting on a goal-setting discipline will help your new (and not-so-new) managers to organize their strategic game plans. Critical but soft goals, such as staff development, are often overlooked because they are difficult to measure. Putting such goals in print with clear action steps makes them concrete, rendering a sense of accomplishment when they are achieved and a greater likelihood that they will be rewarded. Managers with clear goals will be less tempted to become full-time tacticians. Just as important, the process will help you ensure that they are thinking about the right issues and deploying their teams effectively.

Giving Constructive Feedback

It's human nature to avoid confrontations, and most people feel awkward when they have to correct others' behavior or actions. Rookie managers are no exception, and they often avoid addressing important issues with their staff. The typical scenario goes some-thing like this: A staff member is struggling to meet performance goals or is acting inappropriately in meetings. The manager sits back, watches, and hopes that things will magically improve. Other staff members observe the situation and become frustrated by the manager's inaction. The manager's own frustration builds, as she can't believe the subordinate doesn't get it. The straightforward performance issue has now evolved into a credibility problem. When the manager finally addresses the problem, she personalizes it, lets her frustration seep into the discussion with her staff member, and finds the recipient rushing to defend himself from attack.

Most inexperienced managers wait far too long to talk with staff about performance problems. The senior manager can help by creating an environment in which constructive feedback is perceived not as criticism but as a source of empowerment. This begins with the feedback you offer to your managers about their own development. It can be as simple as getting them to tell you where their weaknesses are before they become problematic. After a good performance review, for example, you might say to your new manager, "By all accounts, you have a bright future here, so it's important that we talk about what you *don't* want me to know. What are you feeling least confident about? How can we address those areas so that you're ready for any opportunity that arises?" You'll probably be surprised by how attuned most high performers are to their own development needs. But they are not likely to do much about them unless you put those needs on the table.

More than likely, the feedback your managers have to offer their staffs will not always be so positive or easy to deliver. The key is to foster in them the desire to help their reports achieve their goals. Under those circumstances, even loathsome personal issues become approachable.

One of my clients managed a high-performing senior staff member who was notably unhelpful to others in the department and who resented her own lack of advancement. Instead of avoiding the issue because he didn't want to tell the staff member that she had a bad attitude, the senior manager took a more productive approach. He leveraged his knowledge of her personal goals to introduce the feedback."I know that you're anxious for your first management role, and one of my goals is to help you attain that. I can't do that unless I'm completely honest with you. A big part of management is developing stronger skills in your staff. You aren't demonstrating that you enjoy that role. How can we can work together on that?" No guilt, no admonishment—just an offer to help her get what she wanted. Yet the message was received loud and clear.

A brainstorming session this client and I had about ways to offer critical feedback led to that approach. Often, brainstorming sessions can help rookie managers see that sticky personal issues can be broken down into straightforward business issues. In the case of the unhelpful senior staff member, her attitude didn't really need to enter the discussion; her actions did. Recommending a change in action is much easier than recommending a change in attitude. Never forget the old saw: You can't ask people to change their personalities, but you can ask them to change their behaviors.

Indeed, senior managers should share their own techniques for dealing with difficult conversations. One manager I worked with became defensive whenever a staff member questioned her judgment. She didn't really need me to tell her that her behavior was undermining her image and effectiveness. She did need me to offer her some techniques that would enable her to respond differently in the heat of the moment. She trained herself to respond quickly and earnestly with a small repertoire of questions like,"Can you tell me more about what you mean by that?" This simple technique bought her the time she needed to gather her thoughts and engage in an interchange that was productive rather than defensive. . She was too close to the situation to come up with the technique herself.

Delegating, thinking strategically, communicating—you may think this all sounds like Management 101. And you're right. The most basic elements of management are often what trip up managers early in their careers. And because they are the basics, the bosses of rookie managers often take them for granted. They shouldn't—an extraordinary number of people fail to develop these skills. I've maintained an illusion throughout this article—that only rookie managers suffer because they haven't mastered these core skills. But the truth is, managers at all levels make these mistakes. An organization that supports its new managers by helping them to develop these skills will have surprising advantages over the competition.

Originally published in April 2002
Reprint R0204H

Personalize Your Management Development

NATALIE SHOPE GRIFFIN

Executive Summary

MOST ORGANIZATIONS STRUGGLE with leadership development. They promote top performers into management roles, put them through a few workshops and seminars, then throw them to the wolves. Managers with the ability to survive and thrive are rewarded; those without it are disciplined or reassigned. The problem is, an alarming number of people fall into the second category. This happens not because managers lack skills but because companies fail to realize that there is no single kind of leader-in-training.

In this article, Natalie Shope Griffin, a consultant in executive and organizational development at Nationwide Financial, describes four kinds of managers-in-training, each embodying unique challenges and opportunities.

Reluctant leaders appear to have all the necessary skills to be excellent managers but can't imagine themselves succeeding in a leadership role.

Arrogant leaders have the opposite problem; they believe they already possess all the management skills they'll ever need.

Unknown leaders are overlooked because they don't develop relationships outside of a small circle of close colleagues.

Finally, there are the *workaholics* who put work above all else and spend 100 hours a week in the office.

The author outlines specific training approaches tailored to each type of prospective leader. By focusing on the unique circumstances of individual managers, investing in them early in their careers, offering effective coaching, and providing real-life management experiences, Nationwide's leadership-development program has produced hundreds of successful leaders.

MOST ORGANIZATIONS STRUGGLE with leadership development. They promote their top performers into management roles, put them through a few workshops and seminars, and then throw them to the wolves. In the Darwinian process that follows, those with the ability to survive and thrive are rewarded; those without it are disciplined or reassigned. An alarming number of people fall into the second category.

Why do so many people botch their chances at success? It's not simply that new managers lack the talent or skills for the job. They fail, I've come to believe, because their companies' development approaches fail *them.* I've seen hundreds of leaders-in-training stumble as they attempt to master the difficult and subtle task of management. These prospective managers fall short because companies don't recognize the degree to which personal characteristics, ideologies, or behaviors affect an individual's ability to lead. The truth is, people don't check their individuality at the door before leaping into the great corporate melting pot, nor do they all fit a single leader-in-training profile.

At Nationwide Financial, a 5,000-employee financial services company based in Columbus, Ohio, we've found there are four kinds of people that land in management development programs, each embodying unique challenges and opportunities. First, there are the *reluctant leaders,* who appear to have all the necessary skills to be excellent managers but can't imagine themselves succeeding in a leadership role. *Arrogant leaders* have the opposite problem; they believe they already possess all the leadership skills they'll ever need. They typically lack the empathy and humility characteristic of an effective leader. The third group of people, *unknown leaders,* have the right blend of humility, confidence, and leadership skills, but their talents are overlooked because they fail to develop relationships outside of a small circle of close colleagues. Finally, there are the *workaholics,* the most common profile among our prospective managers. These individuals have been rewarded for putting work above all else and spending excessive hours at the office. Unfortunately, workaholics often lack both the perspective and personality to inspire others.

Identifying these four types of prospective managers and tailoring a specific development path for each has been a boon to Nationwide Financial. By treating potential leaders as individuals—focusing on their unique personalities and circumstances, offering effective coaching, and providing real-life management experiences—Nationwide's leadership development program produced scores of effective managers during a time of rapid growth and expansion when the company needed leadership most.

Responding to the Pipeline Problem

In 1996, the leaders of Nationwide Financial's life insurance operations declared a state of management emergency. Organizational structures had flattened during the economic boom.

As the remaining mid- and senior-level managers were promoted or retired, those who should have replaced them were increasingly unable to lead. Employee satisfaction fell to low levels owing to mediocre frontline management, which suffered from discontent and turnover of its own. The morale problem was exacerbated by the fact that Nationwide had been forced into the expensive practice of hiring talented managers from outside the company; employees hoping for promotion felt passed over. It was clear the company needed to develop a new generation of competent managers from within its own ranks.

To address this worrisome situation, a cross-functional team (of which I later became a member) conducted best-practice research into talent management and leadership development and set about creating a management development process. We agreed that only a rigorously managed program committed to continuous improvement would deliver the kinds of results the company hoped to see. The team opted to make application to the program a matter of choice, rather than a prerequisite for management positions; admission should be a coveted prize so that participants would work hard during the development process. To that end, the admission process mimicked that of a top business school. In addition to submitting a portfolio of documents—performance evaluations, an essay, responses to a questionnaire, a recommendation from a manager—applicants would be screened and interviewed by a team of more senior managers and HR professionals.

The yearlong development program included coaching, mentoring, observing others, hands-on management experience, and training classes backed up by regular feedback sessions. The development focused on the whole person, not just on individual competencies. As the first rounds of participants moved through the program, we noticed that nearly all of them fell into one of four categories. Over the past five years, we've developed specific approaches tailored to each type of prospective leader.

The Reluctant Leader

About 20% of the participants in our program are "reluctant leaders." These employees often have the raw material to make outstanding managers, but they're sabotaged by their own lack of confidence. Their deeply ingrained insecurities manifest themselves in a variety of ways—indecisiveness, risk aversion, and the tendency to avoid conflict. To transform reluctant leaders into strong ones requires helping them change their assumptions about their own abilities, providing them with specific training in decision making and conflict management, and giving them steady doses of encouragement.

Consider Julie, a dedicated employee in our company's call center. A natural leader, she loathed the idea of being one. Though she was an able, intelligent, and compassionate team player, Julie simply didn't believe she had the right to make decisions for others. Moreover, she had worked for too many bosses who routinely took credit for her work. She had convinced herself that being a boss meant being nasty and that altering her style to fit such a mold was neither possible nor appealing. Yet because she was both nurturing and competent, her coworkers naturally turned to her for guidance and feedback. In fact, Julie was already their informal leader. When her manager asked Julie to apply for the job of call center leader and for the leadership development program, Julie reluctantly applied and was accepted to the program. Yet she continued to see herself not as a leader but as a team member who had some additional administrative duties.

It was soon clear that Julie would need to do more than be just another team member. Julie's new team of 15 call-center associates—many of whom were rumored to have been "dumped" in her area by managers who couldn't motivate them or fire them—had a reputation for consistently failing to meet quality and productivity objectives. But still Julie maintained a low profile; faced with decisions, she demurred. A comment she made in a one-on-one coaching session captured her attitude perfectly: "Who am I to make these decisions? I'm not more important than the people I work with. I'll let them decide. They are adults."

In learning to become a good manager, Julie first needed to change her negative assumptions about leadership. In her case, 360-degree feedback was an excellent tool. She scored high in her ability to handle customer problems, get results, and collaborate with peers to solve problems. And people loved her; she received kudos for creating a work environment that was fun and for helping people maintain perspective, even when call volumes peaked. One person wrote: "I would follow Julie wherever she went." Still, criticism followed praise: "I only wish she had enough confidence in her ability to just make decisions and take the lead." Julie was taken aback by the comments: She realized that she was already the empathetic leader she herself had craved, but she also learned that she was a long way from reaching her potential. Sharing the feedback she'd received with her team, Julie explained why she had been reluctant to make decisions. She then solicited the group's expectations of her and outlined her aspirations for them.

To help Julie become more comfortable making decisions and managing conflicts, a mentor created a series of hypothetical problems for her to handle. During coaching sessions, we asked Julie to make and justify decisions about everyday call-center dilemmas. A sample problem went something like this: "A customer calls to complain because he hasn't received the money he requested be withdrawn from his account. You discover that the money was mistakenly wired to another customer's account. The amount is significant, and your boss has been encouraging everyone to find a way to serve the customer without losing money. Do you send the money back to the caller with an apology immediately, or do you try to get the money back from the other customer first?" Julie had to ask herself, "Which has a worse effect on Nationwide's bottom line—the cost of the reimbursement or the cost of going through a collection agency to try to recover the funds?" She chose to reimburse the customer—and when her mentor told her that he would have made the same decision, she felt affirmed in her judgment. The mentor added that it costs Nationwide more to bring in a new customer than to keep an existing one, so you want to nurture those relationships. As Julie became practiced at thinking through managerial decisions in a safe environment, she gradually learned to trust her own thought processes, knowledge of the business, and ability to make good decisions on the spot.

Teaching Julie to manage conflict required a more forceful combination of coaching and hands-on experience. In one instance, an employee felt that a colleague wasn't carrying his weight. Resentful, the employee refused to take up the slack on days when her coworker was away from the office, which placed an additional burden on the other team members. In the past, Julie would not have tried to interfere, simply hoping that the disagreeing parties would sort things out by themselves. But during coaching, she came to understand that such infighting would seriously compromise her department's productivity. She learned how to smooth conflicts by listening to the two opposing sides, then demanding that the combatants focus on their work instead of each other. As part of her development, she was also required to meet with each associate on her team to discuss career goals and progress—including the sensitive subject of performance improvement, a challenge for any risk-averse manager.

Critical to Julie's transformation was an enormous amount of encouragement. During the entire development process, coaches, colleagues, bosses, and mentors were all called upon to provide her with constant, encouraging feedback. The more frequently Julie heard that she had made a good decision or had handled a conflict well, the more confident she became.

More than likely, Julie will never be overly confident, but she has learned to take a stand when necessary and to manage around her self-doubt. The team has responded by exceeding every production measure. Her natural ability to rally others won over even the most skeptical and unmotivated associates, and quality scores rose as the individuals began working as a cohesive team. Just three months after holding the expectations meeting, Julie's team doubled its productivity, lowered its absenteeism, and earned the division's top ranking for quality.

The Arrogant Leader

Only 10% of our participants fall into this category, but they stand out the most because they can be brazen. Arrogant leaders are just as insecure as reluctant ones, but they overcompensate for their self-doubt by convincing themselves that they are already terrific managers. Because they are ambitious self-marketers, most organizations promote them without a second thought. Yet arrogant leaders can wreak havoc on their teams. Transforming such people into capable managers requires a rude awakening in the form of harsh feedback, hands-on practice in empathetic listening and teamwork, and even threats of demotion or dismissal.

Steve, for example, was an extremely competitive and technically competent customer-service team leader who had already been promoted to manager on the strength of his individual performance. Talented at handling difficult customers, Steve's belief in his own capabilities had been reinforced by several promotions from an entry-level position. During our first coaching session, Steve displayed overweening confidence, saying he knew he could do "any management job." In further sessions, we talked about the ways arrogance and ambition can bump a career off track, but he didn't take the hint. Rather, he noted that he'd never recommend one of his own arrogant team members for promotion. When we suggested he might have a similar attitude, he took offense, saying: "Ask anyone I work with. They love working with me. They know I am bored in this job and could do more."

Steve's confrontation with his mistaken self-image began during his 360-degree feedback session, in which he had rated himself as perfect in all categories. The feedback from others was, predictably, the opposite. Scoring low in nearly all areas and hearing that he was considered self-serving came as the first of many shocks.

Clinging to the false image of his own perfection, Steve was slower to make progress than other program participants. Like many arrogant leaders, Steve spent a lot of time laying the groundwork for his next job—scheduling numerous lunches and meetings with executives in other areas of the company—at the expense of his current one. He excused his lack of interaction with his team by saying he trusted his people. But as his team's performance began to suffer, Steve went so far as to ask one of his direct reports to exaggerate the team's production numbers.

This ethical lapse and the attendant humiliation were blessings in disguise, for they provided the breakthrough Steve needed to correct his behavior. A written warning was placed in his file. He was notified that if he didn't turn his performance around, or if he demonstrated any further lapses in judgment, he risked getting fired. During the hard-line coaching session that followed, we pointed out to Steve that his behavior, not that of his team, had led to his current situation, and he needed to take responsibility for it. Steve's self-deceptive armor finally cracked. For the first time, he admitted his fear that people would find out the truth about him—that he was unsure of himself and had no idea how to improve team performance. Steve's manager also took a hand in deconstructing Steve's lifelong assumption that being a leader meant looking good. He told Steve, "You're talented, but you're not fooling anyone. If your behavior doesn't improve, I will never recommend you for promotion, and you may end up being fired."

The next step in Steve's metamorphosis was a forced walk in his associates' shoes. One aspect of his development plan focused on trading places with his direct reports. They were to teach him about managing the workflow, as well as about their other responsibilities and concerns. The more he proved himself able to learn from others, the more successful he would be. This hurdle was huge, for Steve's past actions had cost him the team's trust. At first, associates were reluctant to share ideas, complaints, or anything at all with him.

But as people witnessed Steve's sincere effort to change, heard his thoughtful questions, and saw him listening carefully to their answers, they began to forgive him. A self-deprecating honesty began to replace Steve's phony self-confidence. Because he finally understood that his own success depended on that of his team, he was able to laugh at himself. After graduating from the program, he continued to work extremely hard to change his arrogant habits. Though he's not perfect, Steve is now one of our best mentors—in part because he understands the value of tough love.

The Unknown Leader

Roughly 25% of our program participants are "unknown leaders"—ambitious, highly competent, yet cautious people who form relationships more slowly and tentatively than others. Because they are often introverted, their personal networks are small and they rarely initiate conversations. People don't usually look to them for leadership, and they have little "brand recognition" in their organizations.

To transform unknown leaders into effective managers again requires 360-degree feedback, followed by careful deconstruction of their underlying belief that networking means glad-handing, and that it is a waste of time. It's also effective to force unknown leaders into meetings with new people, but, as is the case with reluctant leaders, this requires a lot of monitoring and support. Additionally, we've found hands-on management experience in an unfamiliar environment to be helpful in bringing unknown leaders out of their shells.

A commissions analyst named John personified the unknown leader.Though he excelled at financial analysis, customer service, and problem solving, John was not one for small talk; his entire focus was on achieving his own results. His fast pace made him seem too busy to entertain questions. He smiled rarely and walked the halls with his head down. His demeanor caused some to conclude he was unapproachable or aloof. Repeatedly passed over for promotion, John was beginning to feel resentful.

His manager noted John's grumblings and suggested he enroll in the leadership development program. The initial 360-degree feedback session was telling. John received average scores and no comments from his peers, simply because no one knew much about him. During the coaching sessions that followed, we asked John how he expected to climb the corporate ladder if nobody knew who he was. Then we discussed his underlying assumptions. To John, quality work spoke for itself. Networking was phony, something that people with less talent had to pursue in order to get noticed. In his view, a relationship was worth having only if the other party shared common ground with him and was capable of a deep conversation. We proposed to John that his assumption that hard work alone merited promotion was outdated. To get ahead, he needed to think of himself as product in need of a brand. Like products in the marketplace, we explained, people are associated with certain characteristics: Joe is brilliant with customers; Jane is creative and innovative; Bill is a master with numbers.

John remained somewhat cynical about being compared to a little-known product, but he saw the point. He responded well to our stark questions: "What have you been doing to move your career forward? Has that been working for you? Why not? What else could you do?" Understanding that he would not get promoted if he didn't begin to network, he decided to try to change. But changing was hard. John couldn't simply flip a switch and become a sociable person. First, he needed to become more comfortable meeting and talking with new people. To this end, we required him to do what Steve had always done as a matter of course—regularly invite more senior managers to lunch. We also required John to interview his own prospective mentors.

We prepared John for these interview sessions by giving him a list of questions—"Tell me about your business?" "What was your career path?" "What do you look for when you're hiring a manager?" and so on—that we also sent to the interviewees. John was surprised to discover that he could hold serious, interesting conversations with total strangers. Like Julie, he learned that he didn't have to totally change his style. In fact, he learned that his natural ability to think analytically and drive to a deeper level in conversations impressed others. And again like Julie, John needed ongoing encouragement, so we made sure that he heard the interviewees' positive comments about him. As these meetings became more habitual for John, he began to look forward to them. In time, he became more approachable, and as a result, his relationships with his coworkers deepened. John began to see that networking was about building authentic relationships.

Another way to bring unknown leaders out of their shells is to give them unfamiliar assignments in new environments. This forces them into close contact with other people—and out of their sphere of technical expertise. This was the case with John. He knew little about the life insurance division he was assigned to take over for a manager on temporary medical leave and was understandably apprehensive. Still, he took the opportunity to build his brand by coaching people, running meetings, overseeing projects, and dealing with problems. Early in this new role, John quickly helped the team deal with a tough customer complaint, prompting his peers to talk about his contribution and good attitude. Eventually, a buzz developed around John—and today, he's considered a top candidate for future management roles.

The Workaholic

By far the largest number of managers in our program—fully 45%—are workaholics. Many have anxiety-driven, addictive personalities, choosing work over and above family, spiritual growth, sports, hobbies, love, or friendship. Of course, workaholism has degrees of severity: There are those people who love their jobs and work long hours without suffering negative consequences. But acute workaholics are like hamsters on a wheel, laboring relentlessly to finish endless daily tasks. Typically extroverts hooked on activity and action, severe workaholics are far more likely to suffer from burnout, stress, and the attendant physical problems—chronic fatigue, heart disease, high blood pressure, and so on. Unfortunately, most companies continue to reward workaholism.

Our own informal research has confirmed that employees respond far more favorably to well-rounded managers with outside interests. They willingly work harder for such managers because they know that when the team is reaching its goals, their personal lives will be respected as well. Our challenge with workaholics, then, is to demonstrate that their modus operandi of working harder rather than smarter is a zero-sum game. Rather than rewarding workaholism, we try to punish it.

Mark, for example, was a classic workaholic. In his first job out of college, he worked 100 hours a week, and his company rewarded him with a string of raises and promotions. By the time Mark's organization was acquired by Nationwide and he came into the leadership development program, he had been a systems project manager for seven years with a track record of positive results. But he had never worked less than 90 hours a week.

During our first coaching session, Mark expressed frustration with some incorrect billing statements issued six weeks earlier. His colleagues didn't take work seriously, he said. He'd lost touch with friends. He blamed his steep weight gain on scant time for exercise. Six-week-old billing issues were his life. Deep down, Mark distrusted everyone. If making up for others' perceived irresponsibility was what was required for his own career advancement, well then, work was his life.

Because workaholics tend to focus on objective measures, 360-degree feedback is not usually an effective training tool for this type of leader. Where participants like Julie, Steve, and John saw areas where they needed to improve, the feedback merely reinforced Mark's belief that he was doing just fine by any objective measure—belying the spiritual, emotional, and physical sacrifices he'd made to become what he sadly was. So we tried another assessment model—the wheel-shaped "healthy leader" model borrowed from professional development consultant Lewis R. Timberlake, which describes the ideal manager as one who is strong in physical, emotional, spiritual, business, family, and social skills. This holistic model proved much more powerful. Having observed that he'd failed in four of the six categories, Mark responded to the kind of wake-up call Scrooge faced: What will people say about you at your funeral?

During the weeks that followed, Mark considered how he'd lost friends, happiness, perspective, and health. With his manager's help, Mark devised a development plan that required him to balance, on a weekly basis, his personal life and work demands. In particular, he was to leave work before 7 pm every day. When Mark wasn't originally able to meet the goal, his manager suggested that working late might cost him consideration for future promotions. The suggestion was clearly absurd to Mark, but he was forced him to ask himself, "Is working so hard really worth risking my job?"

At first, Mark made an awkward attempt to delegate to others. Unaccustomed to the additional work, his associates submitted hurried and incomplete assignments—convincing Mark he'd been right all along. But rather than doing the work himself, Mark chose to talk to his team about his predicament and his attempt to "get a life," to which one team member responded, "Thank goodness. You're too young to be so old and grumpy."

Everyone chipped in to help Mark get his life back. They pushed him out the door before 7. They made certain he reconnected with old college buddies and played golf with them. During these golf outings, Mark's curiosity, creativity, and sense of humor rebounded. At work, he began chatting with coworkers about Ohio State football games and joking around. He started sharing more about himself and taking a genuine interest in people. He also started taking the team to lunch occasionally. He soon found he was better able to set priorities for himself and his staff members; they responded with their own ideas and redoubled energy. Not long after, Mark the golfer and Mark the football fan became Mark the well-rounded senior manager.

In the process of working with the four types of managers, we've learned something about the efficacy of the various development methods we apply. We believe that had we not developed a tailored approach, we would be setting up our managers for failure. While one type of person responds very well to one form of "treatment," the same approach backfires with someone else. Reluctant and unknown leaders require extra doses of support and encouragement, while the threat of harsh consequences makes all the difference with arrogant leaders and workaholics.

Today, we're expanding our leadership development program to the entire company; our goal is eventually to work with all managers in the organization. We have created a process that is turning out leaders that understand how to engage employees, no matter what position they hold in the company, to accomplish great things. Nationwide's culture is becoming one that nurtures talented managers, rather than one that leaves them to struggle through a Darwinian survival game.

Originally published in March 2003
Reprint R0303H

Developing First-Level Leaders

ANDREAS PRIESTLAND AND ROBERT HANIG

Executive Summary

OIL AND ENERGY CORPORATION BP was well aware of the importance of its work group managers on the front lines. Their decisions, in aggregate, make an enormous difference in BP's turnover, costs, quality control, safety, innovation, and environmental performance. There were about 10,000 such supervisors, working in every part of the company—from solar plants in Spain, to drilling platforms in the North Sea, to marketing teams in Chicago. Some 70% to 80% of BP employees reported directly to these lower-level managers. Yet, until recently, the corporation didn't have a comprehensive training program—let alone an official name—for them. For their part, the front-line managers felt disconnected; it was often hard for them to understand how their individual decisions contributed to the growth and reputation of BP as a whole.

In this article, BP executive Andreas Priestland and Dialogos VP Robert Hanig describe how BP in the past five years has learned to connect with this population of managers. After one and a half years of design and development, there is now a companywide name —"first-level leaders"—and a comprehensive training program for this cohort. The authors describe the collaborative effort they led to create the program's four components: Supervisory Essentials, Context and Connections, the Leadership Event, and Peer Partnerships. The design team surveyed those it had deemed first-level leaders and others throughout BP; extensively benchmarked other companies' training efforts for lower-level managers; and conducted a series of pilot programs that involved dozens of advisers.

The training sessions were first offered early in 2002, and since then, more than 8,000 of BP's first-level leaders have attended. The managers who've been through training are consistently ranked higher in performance than those who haven't, both by their bosses and by the employees who report to them, the authors say.

When it comes to translating a company's strategy into results, there's no denying the importance of first-level leaders—those who manage others who *do not* manage others. At BP Group, these leaders oversee operations at retail outlets, manage work crews at chemical plants or refineries, and handle operations at drilling platforms. Some supervise more than ten people; others work with few subordinates in R&D, marketing, or human resources. First-level leaders are the ones who are most responsible for a firm's day-to-day relationships with customers and the bulk of employees. As Harvard professor Linda Hill wrote in *Becoming a Manager,* ". . . managers on the front line are critical to sustaining quality, service, innovation, and financial performance."

Yet high-quality training programs for these people are notoriously difficult to create and maintain. They're typically set up as one- or two-day seminars, and trainees return to the shop floor with little or no follow-up. The process is decentralized: Local HR departments run the programs, and local executives decide which supervisors will attend, based on their subjective assessments or other nonstrategic considerations. As a result, the potential of these managers is left largely unfulfilled, and the entire organization suffers accordingly.

BP, an oil and energy corporation with operations on every continent and more than 100,000 employees, faced precisely this challenge. The company's senior management was aware of the importance of BP's "frontline managers," as it had called them. About 70% to 80% of BP's employees reported directly to them. There were about 10,000 such supervisors around the world (nobody knew the precise number), ranging in age from 25 to 40. They worked in every part of the company, from solar plants in Spain to drilling platforms in the North Sea to marketing teams in Chicago to service stations in China. They brought to their jobs a wide variety of ethnic and cultural backgrounds, education and professional experience, and attitudes about work, the company, and life. Their decisions, in aggregate, made an enormous difference in

BP's turnover, costs, quality, safety, innovation, and environmental performance. They were also the people usually called upon to prevent small problems from becoming full-scale operational disasters. Yet BP didn't have a comprehensive training program for them. The corporation didn't even have a name for these supervisors. In internal HR parlance, they were managers "up to and including Level G," meaning they were separated by six or more hierarchical levels from the topmost executives.

No wonder the frontline managers felt disconnected; it was often hard for them to understand how their individual decisions contributed to the growth and reputation of BP as a whole. A lower-level manager might typically find himself promoted to lead a team with no clear instructions about how to manage people, how to handle appraisals, how to talk about high-stress subjects, or even whom to ask for advice. And if a unit supervisor wanted to move from, say, India to Canada or Australia, no one could be sure that his or her skills and experience could be easily transferred.

"There wasn't any sign that the company wanted to hear from people like me," recalls Ian Mullins, formerly a logistics supply chain manager at BP Chemicals and currently a compliance adviser for the BP Group. "We weren't aiming for the top of the house, but we had leadership ability and ambition—and we felt ignored."

During the past five years, BP has finally learned to connect with this population. There is now a companywide name for the group—"first-level leaders," a title deliberately chosen to emphasize the managers' significance to BP. And there is now a comprehensive training program for this cohort. Since the program was first offered in early 2002, more than 8,000 of the 10,000 first-level leaders (FLLs) have attended training sessions. The attendees, a notoriously tough group, have consistently given the courses average ratings of 8.5 on a scale of one to ten. More important, the managers who've been through training are consistently ranked higher in performance than those who haven't, both by their bosses and by the employees who report to them.

Some of the signature aspects of the program, such as the emphasis on team dynamics and the fact that much of the content is delivered by senior BP executives, have been specifically credited by people throughout BP with helping to make the organization much more collaborative and capable.

Why hadn't BP created such a program before? Because it is much harder than it seems. Indeed, it was only possible because we designed and developed this initiative in a highly participative way—unusual for BP and, we suspect, for many organizations. The year and a half we spent creating the program included surveys of those we had deemed first-level leaders and others throughout BP; extensive benchmarking of other companies' efforts; and a series of design and piloting sessions that involved dozens of advisers and co-creators. We managed to combine all these efforts into a cohesive whole, in which nearly everyone's contribution was not just recognized but also deeply valued.

In the end, this was the broadest and most comprehensive leadership development process BP had ever engaged in; the company invested $1.5 million in its research and development. But it was considered successful enough to have become a model for other such initiatives throughout the company, in part because it represents a $1 million annual savings over the plethora of BP training courses that it has replaced around the world—without creating a backlash. In 2002, BP Group

Chief Executive John Browne honored the FLL program with one of the company's Helios awards for distinguished service to BP.

We both helped to develop the first-level leaders training initiative—of course, as part of a much larger team. The story of that team and its work not only details a best practice in leadership development but also demonstrates that broad change is possible at BP—or, indeed, at any company.

Aspirations and Limits

The project began in early 2000, when a Learning and Development Committee composed of eight senior BP executives was appointed by Lord Browne to rethink the organization's approach to learning and development for its executives and employees. At that time, BP was emerging from a dramatic series of mergers and acquisitions. Three large oil firms—British Petroleum, Amoco, and ARCO—and several smaller companies had joined to form the third-largest oil-producing enterprise in the world. The associated turbulence had taken its toll: Job satisfaction surveys showed that supervisors, team leaders, and other BP managers working on the front lines were unhappy with their own supervisors or their career tracks. As the committee considered this information, its members voiced an aspiration: BP should be composed of bolder, more powerful leaders, from top to bottom.

But how? The committee members were pragmatic enough to realize that they didn't have the answer. They decided to conduct experiments to educate not just themselves but people throughout the company on the fundamental opportunities for learning at BP. The first-level leaders initiative described in this article was one of six experiments the committee oversaw. The others included a project to develop initiatives for better social responsibility and regional governance at BP; a cross-platform learning initiative linking several business subsectors in Asia; a redesign of BP's leadership development program for fast-track executives; an effort to monitor innovation at BP; and a series of "salons"—executive dialogues on wide-ranging but relevant business topics. The experiment in developing first-level leadership was not only a learning and development project but also a moral imperative for BP: If this group was truly the backbone of the company, then the committee felt a responsibility to embrace it.

The committee members agreed to sponsor the first-level leaders initiative but weren't exactly sure how it would unfold. The conventional approach would have been to design a prototype training program, test it once or twice, and then roll it out through the entire corporation. But the committee members understood that a one-size-fits-all program wouldn't take at BP; it wouldn't recognize people's individual jobs, cultures, aspirations, or futures. The group had seen too many well-intentioned, expensive training programs instituted with great fanfare from the top, with no lasting results. At the same time, it understood that BP couldn't keep its current ad hoc, haphazard approach to training lower-level managers. The committee had to find some solution that paradoxically recognized BP's diversity while providing global cohesion.

Andy Inglis, the deputy chief executive of BP Exploration and Production and a member of the Leadership and Development Committee, was the lead sponsor for the first-level leaders initiative. He viewed his involvement as an opportunity to help managers on the front lines understand their piece of the corporate strategy and the drivers for its delivery, as well as the factors behind high performance in their domain—particularly those related to the issues of health, safety, and the environment. Andy's sponsorship was critical; he showed us, for example, how to present our ideas to *his* constituencies—senior and upstream people—more effectively.

Three individuals were tapped to design and develop the initiative—us and project leader Dominic Emery, a senior BP executive with commercial and operational experience. We worked closely with Kate Owen, then BP's head of organizational and learning development, who helped us clarify our thinking and canvass senior executives companywide. She also introduced us to Robert Mountain, an experienced training and development consultant, who briefed us about other companies he had studied that had sought to train their lower-level managers. Cisco, for example, used electronic media extensively, and GE targeted newly appointed managers as part of its comprehensive learning program for supervisors.

It soon became clear that BP had some unique requirements. First, the training initiative would have to embody BP's new, still-evolving corporate culture. Second, while some corporations designed their training initiatives so entire teams could attend two or three sessions over the course of a year, that wasn't practical for BP. We had too many front-line managers scattered in too many places. We would need a more individualized program, in which some people might go to one session and others to two or more. Third, it also wasn't practical for us to use Web-based courses to fill in the gaps between face-to-face sessions, as other companies had done. A fair number of our frontline supervisors worked offshore or in other remote locations not easily accessible by Internet. Fourth, most other companies relied on internal or external training professionals to facilitate their programs. But at BP, we had learned the value of leaders training leaders in our existing executive-level seminars, and we wanted to bring that same concept to the frontline supervisor level. Ultimately, more than 250 senior managers would deliver sections of the FLL courses. Finally, to gain their sponsorship, we needed to assure the members of the Learning and Development Committee of not just superior performance results but potential cost savings as well.

We based the FLL initiative on a theory of corporate change called the "generative spiral model," which was developed by Dialogos founder William Isaacs and colleagues in the organizational learning movement. This model posits that successful organizational innovations start with a small group of "thoughtful, committed citizens" (as Margaret Mead famously put it) that gradually broadens in sponsorship and deepens in awareness. As the relationship between the core group of innovators and various allies becomes more vibrant, the organization's ability to sustain change becomes stronger. By the time the change initiative is extended throughout the company, the organization is ready to accept it.

In the early stages of such a process, it may seem like nothing much is happening, but, in fact, the groundwork is being laid for the change to take hold. By contrast, change initiatives that are rolled out within a month or two of their announcement generally end up failing because they haven't followed a deliberate sequence for building commitment among constituencies, establishing sponsors, and developing the capacity to act in new and different ways.

Getting the System in the Room

One of the first moves suggested by the spiral model is to get the whole system in the room. That is, our design process needed to include representatives from every key constituency—not only the lower-level supervisors we were targeting but also their managers and direct reports. It needed to include people from all of BP's businesses (Exploration and Production, Refining, Trading, Retailing, and Chemical Production); from a range of geographic areas; and from all the organizational heritages (BP, Amoco, ARCO, Castrol, and others). We made sure that all the participants understood one another's backgrounds and perspectives. We gently but relentlessly reached out to people who had reason to be suspicious of us; some managers in the technology groups, for instance, had their own training initiatives that they thought might be threatened by the FLL program. But we persisted, and the extra hassle and costs paid off.

We started by conducting a telephone survey, interviewing about 175 BP managers around the world who played various supervisory roles. Using the data from that survey, and through our network of learning and organizational development professionals across BP, we identified about 250 people spanning all the groups we wanted to include in the program's design process. We brought them together, 30 or 40 at a time, for several one-day workshops between February and April 2001.

The workshops all started with the same statement, generally delivered by Dominic Emery: "First, we're going to take inventory of all the training that is done today for employees below a certain job grade. Second, we want to understand the needs of that group of employees. Third, we want to develop a whole new training program that is, at minimum, cost neutral to our current offerings. This program has to operate globally—and we have only a few months in which to design it. We want you to tell us what you think."

From there, the sessions would move into structured dialogue, in which carefully selected small groups reflected together on the role of the first-level leader, the major challenges such leaders faced, and the development opportunities they should get at BP.

The sessions were energetic and lively. Attendees received materials to read ahead of time—critical insights from previous sessions and summaries and updates as time went on. As we got several of these fact-finding sessions under our belt, we continued to be impressed by the amount of time and effort our participants invested in what was essentially a volunteer initiative. We were especially gratified when some of the senior executive sponsors, who had hesitantly agreed to spend part of a day in these dialogues, became more intrigued. We slotted some time in each session for a senior executive to talk about his or her understanding of leadership and then to take questions. The response from the attendees was so positive that it galvanized the executives themselves. They were starting to feel a pull from the organization—a desire to learn. The sessions also showed that senior leaders could talk to frontline managers not simply as employees but as fellow leaders, thus initiating them directly in the larger community of leadership at BP.

Defining and Understanding the Audience

Since the group we were trying to reach didn't have a name, we had to find one. The titles already in use at

BP—"frontline managers," "supervisors," "team leaders"—had regional (and sometimes negative) connotations. "Team leader" might sound senior in one country and junior in another. In one of the Learning and Development Committee's first dialogues, back in April 2000, it had settled on "first-level leaders." "First" suggested that BP put this group of managers foremost in the company's consciousness. "Level" connoted the hierarchical rank these individuals shared, and "leader" connected this group with BP's keen interest in developing strong leadership.

In all the workshops we conducted early in 2001, we learned a lot about the distinct needs of each group. The first-level leaders wanted a better understanding of the whole corporation and its priorities. For example, increases in oil prices generally led to increases in feedstock costs for BP's refining businesses. Since lower-level supervisors in refining and chemicals typically didn't know the dynamics of the upstream businesses (exploration and production, for instance), they couldn't give customers (or train their staff to give customers) a credible explanation for the pricing change. So, they couldn't explain: "Well, the current wave of demand and the latest OPEC policies have forced the price of oil up. This means extra costs for our own raw materials. We aren't passing on the full costs to you—but we do have to recapture some of them."

The senior executives in our sessions had no idea that the first-level leaders felt so disconnected. Listening to the frontline supervisors talk gave the senior leaders a visceral understanding of the performance gains those managers could reap if they understood how different parts of the organization fit together. It also gave them pause; they realized they would have to stop acting as controllers and gatekeepers, parsing out messages on a need-to-know basis, and become creative partners, nurturing and channeling the enthusiasm and interest of the first-level leaders.

It was also important to hear in those sessions from the hourly staffers who reported to first-level leaders. The workers were more performance-oriented than anyone expected: If there were slackers in an operation, they wanted the first-level leaders to deal with those people promptly—and fire them if necessary.

Moving Slow to Go Fast

We knew that we wanted our training program to teach the first-level leaders the value of being thoughtful and deliberate. We understood this meant we had to live up to the same ideal ourselves. But BP's culture did not traditionally support a reflective pace. Early in 2001, members of the Learning and Development Committee showed their impatience. "Do you really need to bother with all of these workshops?" they asked. We stood our ground, putting ourselves in the uncomfortable position of defending a principle (time for reflection) that our bosses had espoused against their doubts. Here, it made a difference that there were three of us, including one outsider (Robert Hanig) who had seen in other organizations the importance of taking time to reflect. The issue came to a head in a conference call with Andy Inglis. We explained to our chief sponsor how much we had learned in the workshops and the need to take the time to include diverse perspectives.

Andy listened and said, "That's not the way we usually operate. Make sure you do it properly." But then he said something that became a catchphrase for the entire endeavor: "Sometimes you have to go slow to go fast." By the end of the research phase in April 2001, we saw how our deliberation had paid off. We had built up our own capacity to the point where we could competently cross an important threshold—we could turn this initiative into a global program.

Until now, we had assumed that local business units and regions would put their own spin on the main FLL courses. That is, we would develop the basic materials that they would use as they wished, and they would pay for them from their learning and development budgets. But the first-level leaders, their direct reports, *and* their bosses had all agreed: They wanted a truly global program. The design could tolerate some flexibility in implementation, but basically it should be uniform. The first-level leaders, in particular, pushed for a single program. We had not expected this mandate, and it was very welcome, especially when it led directly to the group's next point: The FLL program should get central funding. Otherwise, the first-level leaders said, the program would last only until the next budget cutback. Some divisions would send people; others wouldn't. With central funding, the FLL initiative could replace existing training programs. We took that message to the Learning and Development Committee, and it backed us up, approving our basic ideas and timetable. We were exultant—ready to move directly into designing the curriculum.

Designing the Curriculum

At this point, the process design group hit a snag that almost unraveled the entire program. In canvassing support, we had delayed our work with a critical constituency: BP's extensive staff of learning and development professionals operating in regional offices around the world. We had been reluctant to involve them in early research until we knew for sure that the program would continue. Then, buoyed by our great response from the first-level leaders, we invited some of these professionals to talk with us about integrating their work into the FLL initiative. We expected them to share our enthusiasm. Instead, to our initial annoyance, they balked. Or so it appeared. In fact, they were asking the right questions: "Would this replace our existing programs? How would it meet local needs? How would we be involved?" We realized that, from their perspective, we were imposing yet another new program from BP's central headquarters on their long-decentralized efforts.

To recoup, we returned to our sponsorship-seeking mind-set, talking with them one by one, listening to their concerns. The learning and development professionals wanted a large role, for example, in choosing the trainers for sessions in their geographic areas—a request that, from our perspective, was ideal. It helped that several of BP's most respected regional practitioners became impressed with the quality of the training modules we had developed. Once they saw the value of the project, they recruited other professionals from places like Zimbabwe and China, whom we otherwise would have missed.

With the learning and development professionals on board, we could move into our nuts-and-bolts design process. In June 2001, we convened 15 HR and learning professionals to settle on the curriculum. We did our best to replicate in this group the diversity of the company. We invited people from BP operations in Alaska, Australia, Belgium, China, Germany, Ireland, Zimbabwe, the United States, and the United Kingdom and gathered in a remote British hotel that reminded us of Fawlty Towers. The proprietor had a knack for breaking in at our most intense moments, declaring: "It's teatime now. The scones are on the table." Many of the people who attended will remember that four-day off-site meeting as one of their most creative periods at BP because of the process: We would disagree, hash things out, take a break, talk some more, reach a mutual decision, and start all over again on a new topic.

In the end, we developed six pilot FLL courses, one each in Houston and Chicago in the United States; Port of Spain, Trinidad; Cape Town, South Africa; Aberdeen, Scotland; and Milton Keynes, England. We invited some of the first-level leaders from the early design sessions to each. We also asked some participants from our early sessions to join an informal Sponsorship Group to critique and comment on the pilot courses. This group comprised not just senior executives but also first-level leaders, their bosses, their direct reports, and some staff members from HR and organizational development. The group later helped to recruit local executives and support teams and to organize on-the-ground coordination efforts where the courses were delivered.

"One thing that can't be overstated," says BP's Douglas Frisby, a project manager and a member of the Sponsorship Group, "is the amount of work and effort it took during the implementation phase from local reps—setting the classes up, arranging for people to be there, recruiting trainers, and making sure it was delivered properly. The process design team could not do this without the solid engagement of local people, mostly within the HR and learning-development functions."

In September, the Learning and Development Committee agreed to provide the budget for the first-level leaders initiative. By now the project involved a Web site so that first-level leaders could easily register for the courses, a set of evaluation measures, and a schedule for courses that would start in January 2002. The committee members now held us to our pledge: Could we realize the cost savings we had promised? We said we could, but only if BP as a whole remained committed to the first-level leaders initiative and didn't compete with it. "We'll show that it's possible," we told the committee, "and you sell it to the organization." BP's executive leadership would have to visibly sponsor the FLL initiative or people throughout the company would feel vulnerable supporting it. The committee members agreed, and the conversations turned to logistics. The attack on the World Trade Center had taken place only two weeks before, and business travel was being cut back. We were worried the organization would postpone this global program—but it didn't.

At that same meeting, the committee members had advised us to get a good marketer. We were skeptical at first, but we took their advice and recruited to the team a BP marketing expert, Duncan Blake. This turned out to be crucial, not only for establishing a professional presence but also for deepening our awareness of the FLL population. Getting word out to the entire organization turned out to be more of a challenge than we expected. There was no distribution list that covered the 10,000 or so first-level leaders who work for BP—or even a list of sites. We had to develop our own. We could not simply use the Internet, because BP managers in remote parts of the world, or on offshore oil rigs, don't necessarily have e-mail. Nor do some of our retail staff.

What We Delivered

Having one course of training meant we needed to tie the curriculum tightly into BP's overall learning and development objectives. It helped that we had a rationale for this, laid out in the early days of the initiative by two key high-level sponsors: Kate Owen and John Manzoni, then group vice president, now BP's chief executive of refining and marketing. For the courses to be deemed successful, trainees needed to be able to answer yes to the following questions:

- "Do I have enough awareness of the direction of this organization?" In other words, am I exposed to BP's strategic thinking?
- "Do I have the skills and support I need to deal with the challenges of my immediate business?" In other words, are they giving me what I need to do my job?
- "Do I have the skills and support I need to deal with the leadership challenges I face now?" In other words, can I be the kind of person I need to be in this position?
- "Am I getting enough support and feedback from BP to make the right personal choices about my life and work?" In other words, does BP support my aspirations as well as its own?

To help first-level leaders answer in the affirmative, we developed a training program with four components. Most first-level leaders, we expected, would engage in at least one (and possibly two or three) of them. The four components remain in place today.

SUPERVISORY ESSENTIALS

This segment of the program focuses on the basics of management. First-level leaders are trained on the particulars of project management and technology in their businesses, and they discuss relevant health, environment, safety, and social responsibility issues. This course is delivered through a combination of face-to-face sessions, Web-based programs for those with Internet access, and CD-ROM modules.

CONTEXT AND CONNECTIONS

This two-day session covers BP's overall strategy and its implications for all parts of the global organization. The design is continually revamped as corporate priorities change.

THE LEADERSHIP EVENT

This is the most intensive component of the FLL program, a four-day session for 24 to 36 people. It includes briefings from senior executives, who often incorporate personal stories about their own management dilemmas into their lectures; in-depth training on how to develop better communication, management, and leadership skills, along with sessions on how to build greater confidence and self-awareness; and action learning. Some of the course's role-play exercises promote attentiveness to diversity and inclusion; others teach people how to make less-ambiguous statements or enable more-effective analysis of a team's communication style.

PEER PARTNERSHIPS

This coaching course pairs new first-level leaders with more-experienced colleagues as they progress through the entire FLL training program, thereby laying the groundwork for continued learning and development after the sessions end.

The dialogues built into the courses tend to focus on handling difficult managerial and leadership issues, ranging from local concerns (such as community development near BP's African production sites) to generic topics like the BP brand. "In one [FLL session] that I ran, some people from Exploration and Production couldn't see how the brand related to them," recalls Janet Ashdown, BP's vice president of field supply for retail in Europe. "'A brand is a marketing thing,' they said. But by the end of the conversation, I think they understood that the brand is not just the logo that appears on the gas station pole. It represents the values of the company, the role you play in communities, and the kinds of behaviors that make it easier or more difficult, and more or less expensive, to go into a new market or make a new investment somewhere."

Ashdown also notes that participating in the FLL courses gave senior leaders unprecedented insights into the grass roots of the company. "It's very refreshing to get out and talk to potential leaders. They're a different generation; they see things differently, and they are pretty challenging."

By bringing together people from different parts of BP, the FLL program is also creating unexpected synergies. For example, Castrol Reprocessing Services, a BP maintenance facility, and BP Solar now share a building for some of their technical operations, including Solar's slurry reclamation process, after two first-level leaders met at a Context and Connections session. The program also brings together people who didn't communicate much before; for example, FLL sessions are produced by a combination of local line managers, local HR and organizational development staff, and central HR directors. That in itself has helped learning and organizational development at BP become more consistent and coherent.

The success of the FLL initiative has spawned a similar program for BP's 6,000 senior-level leaders. Within two years, every first- and senior-level leader in the organization will have gone through some form of leadership development. As that population increases, practices such as supplemental meetings and follow-up coaching—FLL reunions, lunches, and briefing workshops—are also taking hold.

BP continues to evaluate the program by surveying the managers who have taken the courses, as well as their superiors and direct reports. The responses consistently show that first-level leaders who have gone through the program perform more effectively than those managers who have not, according to the people they report to and the people who report to them. For two years running, employees supervised by trained first-level leaders have rated their bosses higher by almost 10% in the following areas: communication, interpersonal skills, team leadership, and general management.

BP's success in this initiative has given it the confidence to take leadership development to another level. "We're not finished," Andy Inglis says. "It's been a volatile world for the past two or three years, particularly in the oil and gas industry. Our leadership training needs to match the pace of change around us. We especially need to equip our people to deal with ambiguity and to feel confident in the firm's direction as they go about their daily work. That's a job that is never finished."

Originally published in June 2005
Reprint R0506G

Myth of the Well-Educated Manager

J. STERLING LIVINGSTON

Executive Summary

THIS ARTICLE DISCUSSES THE inability of formal management education programs in both universities and industry to develop explicitly the traits, knowledge, and skills that are essential to career success and leadership in any business organization. In presenting a hard-hitting approach to education and management, this discussion brings us face to face with some of the facts of life about learning in the school room versus learning on the job. Although the author draws on the findings of others, many of the points and ideas expressed are the direct result of his own business observation and experience as a manager, entrepreneur, and teacher.

HOW EFFECTIVELY A MANAGER will perform on the job cannot be predicted by the number of degrees he holds, the grades he receives in school, or the formal management education programs he attends. Academic achievement is not a valid yardstick to use in measuring managerial potential. Indeed, if academic achievement is equated with success in business, the well-educated manager is a myth.

Managers are not taught in formal education programs what they most need to know to build successful careers in management. Unless they acquire through their own experience the knowledge and skills that are vital to their effectiveness, they are not likely to advance far up the organizational ladder.

Although an implicit objective of all formal management education is to assist managers to learn from their own experience, much management education is, in fact, miseducation because it arrests or distorts the ability of managerial aspirants to grow as they gain experience. Fast learners in the classroom often, therefore, become slow learners in the executive suite.

Men who hold advanced degrees in management are among the most sought after of all university graduates. Measured in terms of starting salaries, they are among the elite. Perhaps no further proof of the value of management education is needed. Being highly educated pays in business, at least initially. But how much formal education contributes to a manager's effectiveness and to his subsequent career progress is another matter.

Professor Lewis B. Ward of the Harvard Business School has found that the median salaries of graduates of that institution's MBA program plateau approximately 15 years after they enter business and, on the average, do not increase significantly thereafter.[1] While the incomes of a few MBA degree holders continue to rise dramatically, the career growth of most of them levels off just at the time men who are destined for top management typically show their greatest rate of advancement.

Equally revealing is the finding that men who attend Harvard's Advanced Management Program (AMP) after having had approximately 15 years of business experience, but who—for the most part—have had no formal education in management, earn almost a third more, on the average, than men who hold MBA degrees from Harvard and other leading business schools.

Thus the arrested career progress of MBA degree holders strongly suggests that men who get to the top in management have developed skills that are not taught in formal management education programs and may be difficult for many highly educated men to learn on the job.

Many business organizations are cutting back their expenditures for management training just at the time they most need managers who are able to do those things that will keep them competitive and profitable. But what is taking place is not an irrational exercise in cost reduction; rather, it is belated recognition by top management that formal management training is not paying off in improved performance .

If the current economy wave prompts more chief executives to insist that management training programs result in measurable improvement in performance, it will mark the beginning of the end for many of the programs which industry has supported so lavishly in the past. As Marvin Bower has observed:

> *"One management fad of the past decade has been management development. Enormous numbers*

> *of words and dollars have been lavished on this activity. My observations convince me that, apart from alerting managers more fully to the need for management development, these expenditures have not been very productive.*"[2]

Unreliable Yardsticks

Lack of correlation between scholastic standing and success in business may be surprising to those who place a premium on academic achievement. But grades in neither undergraduate nor graduate school predict how well an individual will perform in management.

After studying the career records of nearly 1,000 graduates of the Harvard Business School, for example, Professor Gordon L. Marshall concluded that "academic success and business achievement have relatively little association with each other."[3] In reaching this conclusion, he sought without success to find a correlation between grades and such measures of achievement as title, salary, and a person's own satisfaction with his career progress. (Only in the case of grades in elective courses was a significant correlation found.)

Clearly, what a student learns about management in graduate school, as measured by the grades he receives, does not equip him to build a successful career in business.

Scholastic standing in undergraduate school is an equally unreliable guide to an individual's management potential. Professor Eugene E. Jennings of the University of Michigan has conducted research which shows that "the routes to the top are apt to hold just as many or more men who graduated below the highest one third of their college class than above (on a per capita basis)."[4]

A great many executives who mistakenly believe that grades are a valid measure of leadership potential have expressed concern over the fact that fewer and fewer of those "top-third" graduates from the better-known colleges and universities are embarking on careers in business. What these executives do not recognize, however, is that academic ability does not assure that an individual will be able to learn what he needs to know to build a career in fields that involve leading, changing, developing, or working with people.

Overreliance on scholastic learning ability undoubtedly has caused leading universities and business organizations to reject a high percentage of those who have had the greatest potential for creativity and growth in nonacademic careers.

This probability is underscored by an informal study conducted in 1958 by W.B. Bender, Dean of Admissions at Harvard College. He first selected the names of 50 graduates of the Harvard class of 1928 who had been nominated for signal honors because of their outstanding accomplishments in their chosen careers. Then he examined the credentials they presented to Harvard College at the time of their admission. He found that if the admission standards used in 1958 had been in effect in 1928, two thirds of these men would have been turned down. (The proportion who would have been turned down under today's standards would have been even higher.)

In questioning the wisdom of the increased emphasis placed on scholastic standing and intelligence test scores, Dean Bender asked, "Do we really know what we are doing?"[5]

There seems to be little room for doubt that business schools and business organizations which rely on scholastic standing, intelligence test scores, and grades as measures of managerial potential are using unreliable yardsticks.

CAREER CONSEQUENCES

False notions about academic achievement have led a number of industrial companies to adopt recruiting and development practices that have aggravated the growing rates of attrition among bright and young managerial personnel. The "High Risk, High Reward" program offered by a large electrical manufacturer to outstanding college graduates who were looking for challenging work right at the beginning of their careers illustrates the consequences of programs that assume that academic excellence is a valid yardstick for use in measuring management potential:

Under this company's program, high-ranking college graduates were given the opportunity to perform managerial work with the assistance of supervisors who were specially selected and trained to assess their development and performance. College graduates participating in the program were assured of promotion at twice the normal rate, provided they performed successfully during their first two years. Since they were to be "terminated" if they failed to qualify for promotion, the program carried high risks for those who participated.

The company undertook this High Risk, High Reward program for two reasons: (1) because its executives believed that ability demonstrated by academic achievement could be transferred to achievement in the business environment, and (2) because they wished to provide an appropriate challenge to outstanding college graduates, particularly since many management experts had contended that "lack of challenge" was a major cause of turnover among promising young managers and professionals.

The candidates for the program had to have a record of significant accomplishment in extra-curricular activities, in addition to a high order of scholarship, and had to be primarily interested in becoming managers. Young men were recruited from a cross section of leading colleges and universities throughout the nation.

Although they were closely supervised by managers who had volunteered to assist in their development, at the end of five years 67% had either terminated voluntarily or had been terminated from their jobs because they had failed to perform up to expectations and were judged not capable of meeting the program's objectives. This rate of attrition was considerably higher than the company had experienced among graduates with less outstanding academic records.

Arrested progress & turnover: Belief in the myth of the well-educated manager has caused many employers to have unrealistic performance expectations of university graduates and has led many employees with outstanding scholastic records to overestimate the value of their formal education. As a consequence, men who hold degrees in business administration—especially those with advanced degrees in management—have found it surprisingly difficult to make the transition from academic to business life. An increasing number of them have failed to perform up to expectations and have not progressed at the rate they expected.

The end result is that turnover among them has been increasing for two decades as more and more of them have been changing employers in search of a job they hope they "can make a career of." And it is revealing that turnover rates among men with advanced degrees from the leading schools of management appear to be among the highest in industry.

As Professor Edgar H. Schein of the Massachusetts Institute of Technology's Sloan School of Management reports, the attrition "rate among highly educated men and women runs higher, on the average, than among blue-collar workers hired out of the hard-core unemployed. The rate may be highest among people coming out of the better-known schools ."[6] Thus over half the graduates of MIT's master's program in management change jobs in the first three years, Schein further reports, and "by the fifth year, 73% have moved on at least once and some are on their third and fourth jobs."[7]

Personnel records of a sample of large companies I have studied similarly revealed that turnover among men holding master's degrees in management from well-known schools was over 50% in the first five years of employment, a rate of attrition that was among the highest of any group of employees in the companies surveyed.

The much publicized notion that the young "mobile managers" who move from company to company are an exceptionally able breed of new executives and that "job-hopping has become a badge of competence" is highly misleading. While a small percentage of those who change employers are competent managers, most of the men who leave their jobs have mediocre to poor records of performance. They leave not so much because the grass is greener on the other side of the fence, but because it definitely is brown on their side. My research indicates that most of them quit either because their career progress has not met their expectations or because their opportunities for promotion are not promising.

In studying the career progress of young management-level employees of an operating company of the American Telephone & Telegraph Company, Professors David E. Berlew and Douglas T. Hall of MIT found that "men who consistently fail to meet company expectations are more likely to leave the organization than are those who turn in stronger performances."[8]

I have reached a similar conclusion after studying attrition among recent management graduates employed in several large industrial companies. Disappointing performance appraisals by superiors is the main reason why young men change employers.

"One myth," explains Schein, "is that the graduate leaves his first company merely for a higher salary. But the MIT data indicate that those who have moved on do not earn more than those who have stayed put."[9] Surveys of reunion classes at the Harvard Business School similarly indicate that men who stay with their first employer generally earn more than those who change jobs. Job-hopping is not an easy road to high income; rather, it usually is a sign of arrested career progress, often because of mediocre or poor performance on the job.

What Managers Must Learn

One reason why highly educated men fail to build successful careers in management is that they do not learn from their formal education what they need to know to perform their jobs effectively. In fact, the tasks that are the most important in getting results usually are left to be learned on the job, where few managers ever master them simply because no one teaches them how.

Formal management education programs typically emphasize the development of problem-solving and decision-making skills, for instance, but give little attention to the development of skills required to find the problems that need to be solved, to plan for the attainment of desired results, or to carry out operating plans once they are made. Success in real life depends on how well a person is able to find and exploit the opportunities that are available to him, and, at the same time, discover and deal with potential serious problems before they become critical.

PROBLEM SOLVING

Preoccupation with problem solving and decision making in formal management education programs tends to distort managerial growth because it overdevelops an individual's analytical ability, but leaves his ability to take action and to get things done underdeveloped. The behavior required to solve problems that already have been discovered and to make decisions based on facts gathered by someone else is quite different from that required to perform other functions of management.

On the one hand, problem solving and decision making in the classroom require what psychologists call "respondent behavior." It is this type of behavior that enables a person to get high grades on examinations, even though he may never use in later life what he has learned in school.

On the other hand, success and fulfillment in work demand a different kind of behavior which psychologists have labeled "operant behavior." Finding problems and opportunities, initiating action, and following through to attain desired results require the exercise of operant behavior, which is neither measured by examinations nor developed by discussing in the classroom what someone else should do. Operant behavior can be developed only by doing what needs to be done.

Instruction in problem solving and decision making all too often leads to "analysis paralysis" because managerial aspirants are required only to explain and defend their reasoning, not to carry out their decisions or even to plan realistically for their implementation. Problem solving in the classroom often is dealt with, moreover, as an entirely rational process, which, of course, it hardly ever is.

As Professor Harry Levinson of the Harvard Business School points out: "The greatest difficulty people have in solving problems is the fact that emotion makes it hard for them to see and deal with their problems objectively."[10]

Rarely do managers learn in formal education programs how to maintain an appropriate psychological distance from their problems so that their judgments are not clouded by their emotions. Management graduates, as a consequence, suffer their worst trauma in business when they discover that rational solutions to problems are not enough; they must also somehow cope with human emotions in order to get results.

PROBLEM FINDING

The shortcomings of instruction in problem solving, while important, are not as significant as the failure to teach problem finding. As the research of Norman H. Mackworth of the Institute of Personality Assessment and Research, University of California, has revealed "the distinction between the problem-solver and the problem-finder is vital."[11]

Problem finding, Mackworth points out, is more important than problem solving and involves cognitive processes that are very different from problem solving and much more complex. The most gifted problem finders, he has discovered, rarely have outstanding scholastic records, and those who do excel academically rarely are the most effective problem finders.

The importance of a manager's ability to find problems that need to be solved before it is too late is illustrated by the unexpected decline in profits of a number of multimarket companies in 1968 and 1969. The sharp drop in the earnings of one of these companies—Litton Industries—was caused, its chief executive explained, by earlier management deficiencies arising from the failure of those responsible to foresee problems that arose from changes in products, prices, and methods of doing business.

Managers need to be able not only to analyze data in financial statements and written reports, but also to scan the business environment for less concrete clues that a problem exists. They must be able to "read" meaning into changes in methods of doing business and into the actions of customers and competitors which may not show up in operating statements for months or even for years.

But the skill they need cannot be developed merely by analyzing problems discovered by someone else; rather, it must be acquired by observing firsthand what is taking place in business. While the analytical skills needed for problem solving are important, more crucial to managerial success are the perceptual skills needed to identify problems long before evidence of them can be found by even the most advanced management information system. Since these perceptual skills are extremely difficult to develop in the classroom, they are now largely left to be developed on the job.

OPPORTUNITY FINDING

A manager's problem-finding ability is exceeded in importance only by his opportunity-finding ability. Results in business, Peter F. Drucker reminds us, are obtained by exploiting opportunities, not by solving problems. Here is how he puts it:

> *"All one can hope to get by solving a problem is to restore normality. All one can hope, at best, is to eliminate a restriction on the capacity of the business to obtain results. The results themselves must come from the exploitation of opportunities. . . . 'Maximization of opportunities' is a meaningful, indeed a precise, definition of the entrepreneurial job. It implies that effectiveness rather than efficiency is essential in business. The pertinent question is not how to do things right, but how to find the right things to do, and to concentrate resources and efforts on them."*[12]

Managers who lack the skill needed to find those opportunities that will yield the greatest results, not uncommonly spend their time doing the wrong things. But opportunity-finding skill, like problem-finding skill, must be acquired through direct personal experience on the job.

This is not to say that the techniques of opportunity finding and problem finding cannot be taught in formal management education programs, even though they rarely are. But the behavior required to use these techniques successfully can be developed only through actual practice.

A manager cannot learn how to find opportunities or problems without doing it. The doing is essential to the learning. Lectures, case discussions, or text books alone are of limited value in developing ability to find opportunities and problems. Guided practice in finding them in real business situations is the only method that will make a manager skillful in identifying the right things to do.

NATURAL MANAGEMENT STYLE

Opportunities are not exploited and problems are not solved, however, until someone takes action and gets the desired results. Managers who are unable to produce effective results on the job invariably fail to build successful careers. But they cannot learn what they most need to know either by studying modern management theories or by discussing in the classroom what someone else should do to get results.

Management is a highly individualized art. What style works well for one manager in a particular situation may not produce the desired results for another manager in a similar situation, or even for the same manager in a different situation. There is no one best way for all managers to manage in all situations. Every manager must discover for himself, therefore, what works and what does not work for him in different situations. He cannot become effective merely by adopting the practices or the managerial style of someone else. He must develop his own natural style and follow practices that are consistent with his own personality.

What all managers need to learn is that to be successful they must manage in a way that is consistent with their unique personalities. When a manager "behaves in ways which do not fit his personality," as Rensis Likert's managerial research has shown, "his behavior is apt to communicate to his subordinates something quite different from what he intends. Subordinates usually view such behavior with suspicion and distrust."[13]

Managers who adopt artificial styles or follow practices that are not consistent with their own personalities are likely not only to be distrusted, but also to be ineffective. It is the men who display the "greatest individuality in managerial behavior," as Edwin E. Ghiselli's studies of managerial talent show, who in general are the ones "judged to be best managers."[14]

Managers rarely are taught how to manage in ways that are consistent with their own personalities. In many formal education and training programs, they are in fact taught that they must follow a prescribed set of practices and adopt either a "consultative" or "participative" style in order to get the "highest productivity, lowest costs, and best performance."[15]

The effectiveness of managers whose personalities do not fit these styles often is impaired and their development arrested. Those who adopt artificial styles typically are seen as counterfeit managers who lack individuality and natural styles of their own.

Managers who are taught by the case method of instruction learn that there is no one best way to manage and no one managerial style that is infallible. But unlike students of medicine, students of management rarely are exposed to "real" people or to "live" cases in programs conducted either in universities or in industry.

They study written case histories that describe problems or opportunities discovered by someone else, which they discuss, but do nothing about. What they learn about supervising other people is largely secondhand. Their knowledge is derived from the discussion of what someone else should do about the human problems of "paper people" whose emotional reactions, motives, and behavior have been described for them by scholars who may have observed and advised managers, but who usually have never taken responsibility for getting results in a business organization.

Since taking action and accepting responsibility for the consequences are not a part of their formal training, they neither discover for themselves what does—and what does not—work in practice nor develop a natural managerial style that is consistent with their own unique personalities. Managers cannot discover what practices are effective for them until they are in a position to decide for themselves what needs to be done in a specific situation, and to take responsibility both for getting it done and for the consequences of their actions.

Elton Mayo, whose thinking has had a profound impact on what managers are taught but not on how they are taught, observed a quarter of a century ago that studies in the social sciences do not develop any "skill that is directly useful in human situations."[16] He added that he did not believe a useful skill could be developed until a person takes "responsibility for what happens in particular human situations—individual or group. A good bridge player does not merely conduct post mortem discussions of the play in a hand of contract; he takes responsibility for playing it."[17]

Experience is the key to the practitioner's skill. And until a manager learns from his own firsthand experience on the job how to take action and how to gain the willing cooperation of others in achieving desired results, he is not likely to advance very far up the managerial ladder.

Needed Characteristics

Although there are no born natural leaders, relatively few men ever develop into effective managers or executives. Most, in fact, fail to learn even from their own experience what they need to know to manage other people successfully. What, then, are the characteristics of men who learn to manage effectively?

The answer to that question consists of three ingredients: (1) the need to manage, (2) the need for power, and (3) the capacity for empathy. In this section of the article, I shall discuss each of these characteristics in some detail.

THE NEED TO MANAGE

This first part of the answer to the question is deceptively simple: only those men who have a strong desire to influence the performance of others and who get genuine satisfaction from doing so can learn to manage effectively. No man is likely to learn how unless he really wants to take responsibility for the productivity of others, and enjoys developing and stimulating them to achieve better results.

Many men who aspire to high-level managerial positions are not motivated to manage. They are motivated to earn high salaries and to attain high status, but they are not motivated to get effective results through others. They expect to gain great satisfaction from the income and prestige associated with executive positions in important enterprises, but they do not expect to gain much satisfaction from the achievements of their subordinates. Although their aspirations are high, their motivation to supervise other people is low.

A major reason why highly educated and ambitious men do not learn how to develop successful managerial careers is that they lack the "will to manage." The "*way* to manage," as Marvin Bower has observed, usually can be found if there is the "*will* to manage." But if a person lacks the desire, he "will not devote the time, energy and thought required to find the way to manage."[18]

No one is likely to sustain for long the effort required to get high productivity from others unless he has a strong psychological need to influence their performance. The need to manage is a crucial factor, therefore, in determining whether a person will learn and apply in practice what is necessary to get effective results on the job.

High grades in school and outstanding performance as an accountant, an engineer, or a salesman reveal how able and willing a person is to perform tasks he has been assigned. But an outstanding record as an individual performer does not indicate whether that person is able or willing to get other people to excel at the same tasks. Outstanding scholars often make poor teachers, excellent engineers often are unable to supervise the work of other engineers, and successful salesmen often are ineffective sales managers.

Indeed, men who are outstanding individual performers not uncommonly become "do-it-yourself" managers. Although they are able and willing to do the job themselves, they lack the motivation and temperament to get it done by others. They may excel as individual performers and may even have good records as first-line managers. But they rarely advance far up the organizational hierarchy because, no matter how hard they try, they cannot make up through their own efforts for mediocre or poor performance by large numbers of subordinates.

Universities and business organizations that select managerial candidates on the basis of their records as individual performers often pick the wrong men to develop as managers. These men may get satisfaction from their own outstanding performance, but unless they are able to improve the productivity of other people, they are not likely to become successful managers.

Fewer and fewer men who hold advanced degrees in management want to take responsibility for getting results through others. More and more of them are attracted to jobs that permit them to act in the detached role of the consultant or specialized expert, a role described by John W. Gardner as the one preferred increasingly by university graduates.[19]

This preference is illustrated by the fact that although the primary objective of the Harvard Business School is to develop managers, less than one third of that institution's graduates actually take first-line management jobs. Two thirds of them start their careers in staff or specialized nonmanagerial positions. In the three-year period of 1967, 1968, and 1969, approximately 10% of the graduates of the Harvard Business School took jobs with management consulting firms and the management service divisions of public accounting firms. A decade earlier, in the three-year period of 1957, 1958, and 1959, only 3% became consultants.

As Charlie Brown prophetically observed in a "Peanuts" cartoon strip in which he is standing on the pitcher's mound surrounded by his players, all of whom are telling him what to do at a critical point in a baseball game: "The world is filled with people who are anxious to act in an advisory capacity." Educational institutions are turning out scholars, scientists, and experts who are anxious to act as advisers, but they are producing few men who are eager to lead or take responsibility for the performance of others.

Most management graduates prefer staff positions in headquarters to line positions in the field or factory. More and more of them want jobs that will enable them to use their analytical ability rather than their supervisory ability. Fewer and fewer are willing to make the sacrifices required to learn management from the bottom up; increasingly, they hope to step in at the top from positions where they observe, analyze, and advise but do not have personal responsibility for results. Their aspirations are high, but their need to take responsibility for the productivity of other people is low.

The tendency for men who hold advanced degrees in management to take staff jobs and to stay in these positions too long makes it difficult for them to develop the supervisory skills they need to advance within their companies. Men who fail to gain direct experience as line managers in the first few years of their careers commonly do not acquire the capabilities they need to manage other managers and to sustain their upward progress past middle age.

"A man who performs nonmanagerial tasks five years or more," as Jennings discovered, "has a decidedly greater improbability of becoming a high wage earner. High salaries are being paid to manage managers."[20] This may well explain in part why the median salaries of Harvard Business School graduates plateau just at the time they might be expected to move up into the ranks of top management.

THE NEED FOR POWER

Psychologists once believed that the motive that caused men to strive to attain high-level managerial positions was the "need for achievement." But now they believe it is the "need for power," which is the second part of the answer to the question: What are the characteristics of men who learn to manage effectively?

A study of the career progress of members of the classes of 1954 and 1955 at the Graduate School of Industrial Management at Carnegie Institute of Technology showed that the need for achievement did not predict anything about their subsequent progress in management.[21] As Harvard Professor David C. McClelland, who has been responsible for much of the research on achievement motivation, recently remarked:

> *"It is fairly clear that a high need to achieve does not equip a man to deal effectively with managing human relationships. . . .*
>
> *"Since managers are primarily concerned with influencing others, it seems obvious that they should be characterized by a high need for power and that by studying the power motive we could learn something about the way effective managerial leaders work."*[22]

Power seekers can be counted on to strive hard to reach positions where they can exercise authority over large numbers of people. Individual performers who lack this drive are not likely to act in ways that will enable them to advance far up the managerial ladder. They usually scorn company politics and devote their energies to other types of activities that are more satisfying to them. But, to prevail in the competitive struggle to attain and hold high-level positions in management, a person's desire for prestige and high income must be reinforced by the satisfaction he gets or expects to get from exercising the power and authority of a high office.

The competitive battle to advance within an organization, as Levinson points out, is much like playing "King of the Hill."[23] Unless a person enjoys playing that game, he is likely to tire of it and give up the struggle for control of the top of the hill. The power game is a part of management, and it is played best by those who enjoy it most.

The power drive that carries men to the top also accounts for their tendency to use authoritative rather than consultative or participative methods of management. But to expect otherwise is not realistic. Few men who strive hard to gain and hold positions of power can be expected to be permissive, particularly if their authority is challenged.

Since their satisfaction comes from the exercise of authority, they are not likely to share much of it with lower-level managers who eventually will replace them, even though most high-level executives try diligently to avoid the appearance of being authoritarian. It is equally natural for ambitious lower-level managers who have a high need for power themselves to believe that better results would be achieved if top management shared more authority with them, even though they, in turn, do not share much of it with their subordinates.

One of the least rational acts of business organizations is that of hiring managers who have a high need to exercise authority, and then teaching them that authoritative methods are wrong and that they should be consultative or participative. It is a serious mistake to teach managers that they should adopt styles that are artificial and inconsistent with their unique personalities. Yet this is precisely what a large number of business organizations are doing; and it explains, in part, why their management development programs are not effective.

What managerial aspirants should be taught is how to exercise their authority in a way that is appropriate to the characteristics of the situation and the people involved. Above all, they need to learn that the real source of their power is their own knowledge and skill, and the strength of their own personalities, not the authority conferred on them by their positions. They need to know that overreliance on the traditional authority of their official positions is likely to be fatal to their career aspirations because the effectiveness of this kind of authority is declining everywhere—in the home, in the church, and in the state as well as in business.

More than authority to hire, promote, and fire is required to get superior results from most subordinates. To be effective, managers must possess the authority that comes with knowledge and skill, and be able to exercise the charismatic authority that is derived from their own personalities.

When they lack the knowledge or skill required to perform the work, they need to know how to share their traditional authority with those who know what has to be done to get results. When they lack the charisma needed to get the willing cooperation of those on whom they depend for performance, they must be able to share their traditional authority with the informal leaders of the group, if any exist.

But when they know what has to be done and have the skill and personality to get it done, they must exercise their traditional authority in whatever way is necessary to get the results they desire. Since a leader cannot avoid the exercise of authority, he must understand the nature and limitations of it, and be able to use it in an appropriate manner. Equally important, he must avoid trying to exercise authority he does not, in fact, possess.

THE CAPACITY FOR EMPATHY

Mark Van Doren once observed that an educated man is one "who is able to use the intellect he was born with: the intellect, and whatever else is important."[24] At the top of the list of "whatever else is important" is the third characteristic necessary in order to manage other people successfully. Namely, it is the capacity for empathy or the ability to cope with the emotional reactions that inevitably occur when people work together in an organization.

Many men who have more than enough abstract intelligence to learn the methods and techniques of management fail because their affinity with other people is almost entirely intellectual or cognitive. They may have "intellectual empathy" but may not be able to sense or identify the unverbalized emotional feelings which strongly influence human behavior.[25] They are emotion-blind just as some men are color-blind.

Such men lack what Norman L. Paul describes as "affective empathy."[26] And since they cannot recognize unexpressed emotional feelings, they are unable to learn from their own experience how to cope with the emotional reactions that are crucial in gaining the willing cooperation of other people.

Many men who hold advanced degrees in management are emotion-blind. As Schein has found, they often are "mired in the code of rationality" and, as a consequence, "undergo a rude shock" on their first jobs.[27] After interviewing dozens of recent graduates of the Sloan School of Management at MIT, Schein reported that "they talk like logical men who have stumbled into a cell of irrational souls," and he added:

> *"At an emotional level, ex-students resent the human emotions that make a company untidy. . . . [Few] can accept without pain the reality of the organization's human side. Most try to wish it away, rather than work in and around it. . . . If a graduate happens to have the capacity to accept, maybe to love, human organization, this gift seems directly related to his potential as a manager or executive."*[28]

Whether managers can be taught in the classroom how to cope with human emotions is a moot point. There is little reason to believe that what is now taught in psychology classes, human relations seminars, and sensitivity training programs is of much help to men who are "mired in the code of rationality" and who lack "affective empathy."

Objective research has shown that efforts to sensitize supervisors to the feelings of others not only often have failed to improve performance, but in some cases have made the situation worse than it was before.[29] Supervisors who are unable "to tune in empathically" on the emotional feelings aroused on the job are not likely to improve their ability to empathize with others in the classroom.[30]

Indeed, extended classroom discussions about what other people should do to cope with emotional situations may well inhibit rather than stimulate the development of the ability of managers to cope with the emotional reactions they experience on the job.

Conclusion

Many highly intelligent and ambitious men are not learning from either their formal education or their own experience what they most need to know to build successful careers in management.

Their failure is due, in part, to the fact that many crucial managerial tasks are not taught in management education programs but are left to be learned on the job, where few managers ever master them because no one teaches them how. It also is due, in part, to the fact that what takes place in the classroom often is miseducation that inhibits their ability to learn from their experience. Commonly, they learn theories of management that cannot be applied successfully in practice, a limitation many of them discover only through the direct experience of becoming a line executive and meeting personally the problems involved.

Some men become confused about the exercise of authority because they are taught only about the traditional authority a manager derives from his official position—a type of authority that is declining in effectiveness everywhere. A great many become inoculated with an "anti-leadership vaccine" that arouses within them intense negative feelings about authoritarian leaders, even though a leader cannot avoid the exercise of authority any more than he can avoid the responsibility for what happens to his organization.

Since these highly educated men do not learn how to exercise authority derived from their own knowledge and skill or from the charisma of their own personalities, more and more of them avoid responsibility for the productivity of others by taking jobs that enable them to act in the detached role of the consultant or specialized expert. Still others impair their effectiveness by adopting artificial managerial styles that are not consistent with their own unique personalities but give them the appearance of being "consultative" or "participative," an image they believe is helpful to their advancement up the managerial ladder.

Some managers who have the intelligence required to learn what they need to know fail because they lack "whatever else is important," especially "affective empathy" and the need to develop and stimulate the productivity of other people. But the main reason many highly educated men do not build successful managerial careers is that they are not able to learn from their own firsthand experience what they need to know to gain the willing cooperation of other people. Since they have not learned how to observe their environment firsthand or to assess feedback from their actions, they are poorly prepared to learn and grow as they gain experience.

Alfred North Whitehead once observed that "the secondhandedness of the learned world is the secret of its mediocrity."[31] Until managerial aspirants are taught to learn from their own firsthand experience, formal management education will remain secondhanded. And its secondhandedness is the real reason why the well-educated manager is a myth.

Notes

1. Lewis B. Ward, *Analysis of 1969 Alumni Questionnaire Returns,* an unpublished report to the Faculty, Harvard Business School, 1970.
2. Marvin Bower, *The Will to Manage* (New York, McGraw-Hill Book Company, Inc., 1966), p. 171.
3. Gordon L. Marshall, "Predicting Executive Achievement," unpublished doctoral thesis, Harvard Business School, June 1964.
4. Eugene E. Jennings, *The Mobile Manager* (Ann Arbor, Bureau of Industrial Relations, University of Michigan, Graduate School of Business Administration, 1967), p. 21.
5. Quoted in Anthony G. Athos and Lewis B. Ward, "Corporations and College Recruiting: A Study of Perceptions" (unpublished study being prepared for the Division of Research, Harvard Business School), p. 14.
6. Edgar H. Schein, "How Graduates Scare Bosses," *Careers Today,* Volume 1, Number 1, p. 95.
7. Ibid., p. 90.
8. David E. Berlew and Douglas T. Hall, "The Management of Tension in Organization: Some Preliminary Findings," *Industrial Management Review,* Fall 1964, p. 36.
9. Schein, op. cit., p. 90.
10. Harry Levinson, *Executive Stress* (New York, Harper & Row, Publishers, 1970), pp. 109–110.
11. Norman H. Mackworth, "Originality," in *The Discovery of Talent,* edited by Dael Wolfle (Cambridge, Massachusetts, Harvard University Press, 1969), p. 242.
12. Peter F. Drucker, *Managing For Results* (New York, Harper & Row, Publishers, 1964), p. 5.
13. Rensis Likert, *New Patterns of Management* (New York, McGraw-Hill Book Company, Inc., 1969), p. 90.
14. Edwin E. Ghiselli, "Managerial Talent," in Wolfle, op. cit., p. 236.

15. Rensis Likert, *The Human Organization* (New York, McGraw-Hill Book Company Inc., 1967), p. 11.
16. Elton Mayo, *The Social Problems of an Industrial Civilization* (Boston, Division of Research, Harvard Business School, 1945), p. 19.
17. Ibid., p. 32.
18. Bower, op. cit., p. 6.
19. John W. Gardner, "The Anti-Leadership Vaccine," *1965 Annual Report,* Carnegie Corporation of New York.
20. Jennings, op. cit., p. 15.
21. William R. Dill, "GSIA Alumni—Their Progress and Their Goals," Carnegie Institute of Technology, 1962, p. 9.
22. David C. McClelland, "The Two Faces of Power," unpublished manuscript, Harvard University, September 15, 1968, p. 2.
23. Harry Levinson, "On Becoming a Middle-Aged Manager," HBR July–August 1969, p. 53.
24. Mark Van Doren, *Liberal Education* (Boston, Beacon Press, 1967), p. 13.
25. Norman L. Paul, "The Use of Empathy in the Resolution of Grief," *Perspectives in Biology and Medicine,* Autumn 1967 (The University of Chicago Press), p. 155.
26. Ibid., p. 155.
27. Schein, op. cit., p. 92.
28. Ibid., p. 90.
29. See E.A. Fleishmann, E.F. Harris, and H.E. Burt, *Leadership and Supervision in Industry: An Evaluation of a Supervisory Training Program,* Monograph No. 33 (Columbus, Ohio, Bureau of Education Research, The Ohio State University, 1955).
30. Paul, op. cit., pp. 156–157.
31. Alfred North Whitehead, *Aims of Education and Other Essays* (New York, The Macmillan Company, 1929), p. 79.

Originally published in January 1971
Reprint 71108

Becoming the Boss

LINDA A. HILL

Executive Summary

EVEN FOR THE MOST GIFTED individuals, the process of becoming a leader is an arduous, albeit rewarding, journey of continuous learning and self-development. The initial test along the path is so fundamental that we often overlook it: becoming a boss for the first time. That's a shame, because the trials involved in this rite of passage have serious consequences for both the individual and the organization.

For a decade and a half, the author has studied people—particularly star performers—making major career transitions to management. As firms have become leaner and more dynamic, new managers have described a transition that gets more difficult all the time. But the transition is often harder than it need be because of managers' misconceptions about their role. Those who can acknowledge their misconceptions have a far greater chance of success.

For example, new managers typically assume that their position will give them the authority and freedom to do what they think is best. Instead, they find themselves enmeshed in a web of relationships with subordinates, bosses, peers, and others, all of whom make relentless and often conflicting demands. "You really are not in control of anything," says one new manager.

Another misconception is that new managers are responsible only for making sure that their operations run smoothly. But new managers also need to realize they are responsible for recommending and initiating changes—some of them in areas outside their purview—that will enhance their groups' performance.

Many new managers are reluctant to ask for help from their bosses. But when they do ask (often because of a looming crisis), they are relieved to find their superiors more tolerant of their questions and mistakes than they had expected.

EVEN FOR THE MOST GIFTED individuals, the process of becoming a leader is an arduous, albeit rewarding, journey of continuous learning and self-development. The initial test along the path is so fundamental that we often overlook it: becoming a boss for the first time. That's a shame, because the trials involved in this rite of passage have serious consequences for both the individual and the organization.

Executives are shaped irrevocably by their first management positions. Decades later, they recall those first months as transformational experiences that forged their leadership philosophies and styles in ways that may continue to haunt and hobble them throughout their careers. Organizations suffer considerable human and financial costs when a person who has been promoted because of strong individual performance and qualifications fails to adjust successfully to management responsibilities.

The failures aren't surprising, given the difficulty of the transition. Ask any new manager about the early days of being a boss—indeed, ask any senior executive to recall how he or she felt as a new manager. If you get an honest answer, you'll hear a tale of disorientation and, for some, overwhelming confusion. The new role didn't feel anything like it was supposed to. It felt too big for any one person to handle. And whatever its scope, it sure didn't seem to have anything to do with leadership.

In the words of one new branch manager at a securities firm: "Do you know how hard it is to be the boss when you are so out of control? It's hard to verbalize. It's the feeling you get when you have a child. On day X minus 1, you still don't have a child. On day X, all of a sudden you're a mother or a father and you're supposed to know everything there is to know about taking care of a kid."

Given the significance and difficulty of this first leadership test, it's surprising how little attention has been paid to the experiences of new managers and the challenges they face. The shelves are lined with books describing effective and successful leaders. But very few address the challenges of learning to lead, especially for the first-time manager.

For the past 15 years or so, I've studied people making major career transitions to management, focusing in particular on the star performer who is promoted to manager. My original ambition was to provide a forum for new managers to speak in their own words about what it means to learn to manage. I initially followed 19 new managers over the course of their first year in an effort to get a rare glimpse into their subjective experience: What did they find most difficult? What did they need to learn? How did they go about learning it? What resources did they rely upon to ease the transition and master their new assignments?

Since my original research, which I described in the first edition of *Becoming a Manager,* published in 1992, I've continued to study the personal transformation involved when someone becomes a boss. I've written case studies about new managers in a variety of functions and industries and have designed and led new-manager leadership programs for companies and not-for-profit organizations. As firms have become leaner and more dynamic—with different units working together to offer integrated products and services and with companies working with suppliers, customers, and competitors in an array of strategic alliances—new managers have described a transition that gets harder all the time.

Let me emphasize that the struggles these new managers face represent the norm, not the exception. These aren't impaired managers operating in dysfunctional organizations. They're ordinary people facing ordinary adjustment problems. The vast majority of them survive the transition and learn to function in their new role.

But imagine how much more effective they would be if the transition were less traumatic.

To help new managers pass this first leadership test, we need to help them understand the essential nature of their role—what it truly means to be in charge. Most see themselves as managers and leaders; they use the rhetoric of leadership; they certainly feel the burdens of leadership. But they just don't get it.

Why Learning to Manage Is So Hard

One of the first things new managers discover is that their role, by definition a stretch assignment, is even more demanding than they'd anticipated. They are surprised to learn that the skills and methods required for success as an individual contributor and those required for success as a manager are starkly different—and that there is a gap between their current capabilities and the requirements of the new position.

In their prior jobs, success depended primarily on their personal expertise and actions. As managers, they are responsible for setting and implementing an agenda for a whole group, something for which their careers as individual performers haven't prepared them.

Take the case of Michael Jones, the new securities-firm branch manager I just mentioned. (The identities of individuals cited in this article have been disguised.) Michael had been a broker for 13 years and was a stellar producer, one of the most aggressive and innovative professionals in his region. At his company, new branch managers were generally promoted from the ranks on the basis of individual competence and achievements, so no one was surprised when the regional director asked him to consider a management career. Michael was confident he understood what it took to be an effective manager. In fact, on numerous occasions he had commented that if he had been in charge, he would have been willing and able to fix things and make life better in the branch. After a month in his new role, however, he was feeling moments of intense panic; it was harder than he had imagined to get his ideas implemented. He realized he had given up his "security blanket" and there was no turning back.

Michael's reaction, although a shock to him, isn't unusual. Learning to lead is a process of learning by doing. It can't be taught in a classroom. It is a craft primarily acquired through on-the-job experiences—especially adverse experiences in which the new manager, working beyond his current capabilities, proceeds by trial and error. Most star individual performers haven't made many mistakes, so this is new for them. Furthermore, few managers are aware, in the stressful, mistake-making moments, that they are learning. The learning occurs incrementally and gradually.

As this process slowly progresses—as the new manager unlearns a mind-set and habits that have served him over a highly successful early career—a new professional identity emerges. He internalizes new ways of thinking and being and discovers new ways of measuring success and deriving satisfaction from work. Not surprisingly, this kind of psychological adjustment is taxing. As one new manager notes, "I never knew a promotion could be so painful."

Painful—and stressful. New managers inevitably ponder two questions: "Will I like management?" and "Will I be good at management?" Of course, there are no immediate answers; they come only with experience. And these two questions are often accompanied by an even more unsettling one: "Who am I becoming?"

A New Manager's Misconceptions

Becoming a boss is difficult, but I don't want to paint an unrelentingly bleak picture. What I have found in my research is that the transition is often harder than it need be because of new managers' misconceptions about their role. Their ideas about what it means to be a manager hold some truth. But, because these notions are simplistic and incomplete, they create false expectations that individuals struggle to reconcile with the reality of managerial life. By acknowledging the following misconceptions—some of which rise almost to the level of myth in their near-universal acceptance—new managers have a far greater chance of success. (For a comparison of the misconceptions and the reality, see the exhibit "Why New Managers Don't Get It.")

MANAGERS WIELD SIGNIFICANT AUTHORITY

When asked to describe their role, new managers typically focus on the rights and privileges that come with being the boss. They assume the position will give them more authority and, with that, more freedom and autonomy to do what they think is best for the organization. No longer, in the words of one, will they be "burdened by the unreasonable demands of others."

New managers nursing this assumption face a rude awakening. Instead of gaining new authority, those I have studied describe finding themselves hemmed in by interdependencies. Instead of feeling free, they feel constrained, especially if they were accustomed to the relative independence of a star performer. They are enmeshed in a web of relationships—not only with subordinates but also with bosses, peers, and others inside

Why New Managers Don't Get It

Beginning managers often fail in their new role, at least initially, because they come to it with misconceptions or myths about what it means to be a boss. These myths, because they are simplistic and incomplete, lead new managers to neglect key leadership responsibilities.

	Myth	Reality
Defining characteristic of the new role:	**Authority** “Now I will have the freedom to implement my ideas.”	**Interdependency** “It's humbling that someone who works for me could get me fired.”
Source of power:	**Formal authority** “I will finally be on top of the ladder.”	**“Everything but”** “Folks were wary, and you really had to earn it.”
Desired outcome:	**Control** “I must get compliance from my subordinates.”	**Commitment** “Compliance does not equal commitment.”
Managerial focus:	**Managing one-on-one** “My role is to build relationships with individual subordinates.”	**Leading the team** “I need to create a culture that will allow the group to fulfill its potential.”
Key challenge:	**Keeping the operation in working order** “My job is to make sure the operation runs smoothly.”	**Making changes that will make the team perform better** “I am responsible for initiating changes to enhance the group's performance.”

and outside the organization, all of whom make relentless and often conflicting demands on them. The resulting daily routine is pressured, hectic, and fragmented.

"The fact is that you really are not in control of anything," says one new manager. "The only time I am in control is when I shut my door, and then I feel I am not doing the job I'm supposed to be doing, which is being with the people." Another new manager observes: "It's humbling that someone who works for me could get me fired."

The people most likely to make a new manager's life miserable are those who don't fall under her formal authority: outside suppliers, for example, or managers in another division. Sally McDonald, a rising star at a chemical company, stepped into a product development position with high hopes, impeccable credentials as an individual performer, a deep appreciation for the company's culture—and even the supposed wisdom gained in a leadership development course. Three weeks later, she observed grimly: "Becoming a manager is not about becoming a boss. It's about becoming a hostage. There are many terrorists in this organization that want to kidnap me."

Until they give up the myth of authority for the reality of negotiating interdependencies, new managers will not be able to lead effectively. As we have seen, this goes beyond managing the team of direct reports and requires managing the context within which the team operates. Unless they identify and build effective relationships with the key people the team depends upon, the team will lack the resources necessary to do its job.

Even if new managers appreciate the importance of these relationships, they often ignore or neglect them and focus instead on what seems like the more immediate task of leading those closest to them: their subordinates. When they finally do accept their network-builder role, they often feel overwhelmed by its demands. Besides, negotiating with these other parties from a position of relative weakness—for that's often the plight of new managers at the bottom of the hierarchy—gets tiresome.

But the dividends of managing the interdependencies are great. While working in business development at a large U.S. media concern, Winona Finch developed a business plan for launching a Latin American edition of the company's U.S. teen magazine. When the project got tentative approval, Finch asked to manage it. She and her team faced a number of obstacles. International projects were not favored by top management, and before getting final funding, Finch would need to secure agreements with regional distributors representing 20% of the Latin American market—not an easy task for an untested publication competing for scarce newsstand space. To control costs, her venture would have to rely on the sales staff of the Spanish-language edition of the company's flagship women's magazine, people who were used to selling a very different kind of product.

Winona had served a stint as an acting manager two years before, so despite the morass of detail she had to deal with in setting up the new venture, she understood the importance of devoting time and attention to managing relationships with her superiors and peers. For example, she compiled biweekly executive notes from her department heads that she circulated to executives at headquarters. To enhance communication with the women's magazine, she initiated regular Latin American board meetings at which top worldwide executives from both the teen and women's publications could discuss regional strategy.

Her prior experience notwithstanding, she faced the typical stresses of a new manager: "It's like you are in final exams 365 days a year," she says. Still, the new edition was launched on schedule and exceeded its business plan forecasts.

AUTHORITY FLOWS FROM THE MANAGER'S POSITION

Don't get me wrong: Despite the interdependencies that constrain them, new managers do wield some power. The problem is that most of them mistakenly believe their power is based on the formal authority that comes with their now lofty—well, relatively speaking—position in the hierarchy. This operating assumption leads many to adopt a hands-on, autocratic approach, not because they are eager to exercise their new power over people but because they believe it is the most effective way to produce results.

New managers soon learn, however, that when direct reports are told to do something, they don't necessarily respond. In fact, the more talented the subordinate, the less likely she is to simply follow orders. (Some new managers, when pressed, admit that they didn't always listen to their bosses either.)

After a few painful experiences, new managers come to the unsettling realization that the source of their power is, according to one, "everything but" formal authority. That is, authority emerges only as the manager establishes credibility with subordinates, peers, and superiors. "It took me three months to realize I had no effect on many of my people," recalls one manager I followed. "It was like I was talking to myself."

Many new managers are surprised by how difficult it is to earn people's respect and trust. They are shocked, and even insulted, that their expertise and track record don't speak for themselves. My research shows that many also aren't aware of the qualities that contribute to credibility.

They need to demonstrate their *character*—the intention to do the right thing. This is of particular importance to subordinates, who tend to analyze every statement and nonverbal gesture for signs of the new boss's motives. Such scrutiny can be unnerving. "I knew I was a good guy, and I kind of expected people to accept me immediately for what I was," says one new manager. "But folks were wary, and you really had to earn it."

They need to demonstrate their *competence*—knowing how to do the right thing. This can be problematic, because new managers initially feel the need to prove their technical knowledge and prowess, the foundations of their success as individual performers. But while evidence of technical competence is important in gaining subordinates' respect, it isn't ultimately the primary area of competence that direct reports are looking for.

When Peter Isenberg took over the management of a trading desk in a global investment bank, he oversaw a group of seasoned, senior traders. To establish his credibility, he adopted a hands-on approach, advising traders to close down particular positions or try different trading strategies. The traders pushed back, demanding to know the rationale for each directive. Things got uncomfortable. The traders' responses to their new boss's comments became prickly and terse. One day, Isenberg, who recognized his lack of knowledge about foreign markets, asked one of the senior people a simple question about pricing. The trader stopped what he was doing for several minutes to explain the issue and offered to discuss the matter further at the end of the day. "Once I stopped talking all the time and began to listen, people on the desk started to educate me about the job and, significantly, seemed to question my calls far less," Isenberg says.

The new manager's eagerness to show off his technical competence had undermined his credibility as a manager and leader. His eagerness to jump in and try to solve problems raised implicit questions about his managerial competence. In the traders' eyes, he was becoming a micromanager and a "control freak" who didn't deserve their respect.

Finally, new managers need to demonstrate their *influence*—the ability to deliver and execute the right thing. There is "nothing worse than working for a powerless boss," says a direct report of one new manager I studied. Gaining and wielding influence within the organization is particularly difficult because, as I have noted, new managers are the "little bosses" of the organization. "I was on top of the world when I knew I was finally getting promoted," one new manager says. "I felt like I would be on the top of the ladder I had been climbing for years. But then I suddenly felt like I was at the bottom again—except this time it's not even clear what the rungs are and where I am climbing to."

Once again, we see a new manager fall into the trap of relying too heavily on his formal authority as his source of influence. Instead, he needs to build his influence by creating a web of strong, interdependent relationships, based on credibility and trust, throughout his team and the entire organization—one strand at a time.

MANAGERS MUST CONTROL THEIR DIRECT REPORTS

Most new managers, in part because of insecurity in an unfamiliar role, yearn for compliance from their subordinates. They fear that if they don't establish this early on, their direct reports will walk all over them. As a means of gaining this control, they often rely too much on their formal authority—a technique whose effectiveness is, as we have seen, questionable at best.

But even if they are able to achieve some measure of control, whether through formal authority or authority earned over time, they have achieved a false victory. Compliance does not equal commitment. If people aren't committed, they won't take the initiative. And if subordinates aren't taking the initiative, the manager can't delegate effectively. The direct reports won't take the calculated risks that lead to the continuous change and improvement required by today's turbulent business environment.

Winona Finch, who led the launch of the teen magazine in Latin America, knew she faced a business challenge that would require her team's total support. She had in fact been awarded the job in part because of her personal style, which her superiors hoped would compensate for her lack of experience in the Latin American market and in managing profit-and-loss responsibilities. In addition to being known as a clear thinker, she had a warm and personable way with people. During the project, she successfully leveraged these natural abilities in developing her leadership philosophy and style.

Instead of relying on formal authority to get what she wanted from her team, she exercised influence by creating a culture of inquiry. The result was an organization in which people felt empowered, committed, and accountable for fulfilling the company's vision. "Winona was easygoing and fun," a subordinate says. "But she would ask and ask and ask to get to the bottom of something. You would say something to her, she would say it back to you, and that way everyone was 100% clear on what we were talking about. Once she got the information and knew what you were doing, you had to be consistent. She would say, 'You told me X; why are you doing Y? I'm confused.'" Although she was demanding, she didn't demand that people do things her way. Her subordinates were committed to the team's goals because they were empowered, not ordered, to achieve them.

The more power managers are willing to share with subordinates in this way, the more influence they tend to command. When they lead in a manner that allows their people to take the initiative, they build their own credibility as managers.

MANAGERS MUST FOCUS ON FORGING GOOD INDIVIDUAL RELATIONSHIPS

Managing interdependencies and exercising informal authority derived from personal credibility require new managers to build trust, influence, and mutual expectations with a wide array of people. This is often achieved by establishing productive personal relationships. Ultimately, however, the new manager must figure out how to harness the power of a team. Simply focusing on one-on-one relationships with members of the team can undermine that process.

During their first year on the job, many new managers fail to recognize, much less address, their team-building responsibilities. Instead, they conceive of their people-management role as building the most effective relationships they can with each individual subordinate, erroneously equating the management of their team with managing the individuals on the team.

They attend primarily to individual performance and pay little or no attention to team culture and performance. They hardly ever rely on group forums for identifying and solving problems. Some spend too much time with a small number of trusted subordinates, often those who seem most supportive. New managers tend to handle issues, even those with teamwide implications, one-on-one. This leads them to make decisions based on unnecessarily limited information.

In his first week as a sales manager at a Texas software company, Roger Collins was asked by a subordinate for an assigned parking spot that had just become available. The salesman had been at the company for years, and Collins, wanting to get off to a good start with this veteran, said, "Sure, why not?" Within the hour, another salesman, a big moneymaker, stormed into Collins's office threatening to quit. It seems the shaded parking spot was coveted for pragmatic and symbolic reasons, and the beneficiary of Collins's casual gesture was widely viewed as incompetent. The manager's decision was unfathomable to the star.

Collins eventually solved what he regarded as a trivial management problem—"This is not the sort of thing I'm supposed to be worrying about," he said—but he began to recognize that every decision about individuals affected the team. He had been working on the assumption that if he could establish a good relationship with each person who reported to him, his whole team would function smoothly. What he learned was that supervising each individual was not the same as leading the team.

In my research, I repeatedly hear new managers describe situations in which they made an exception for one subordinate—usually with the aim of creating a positive relationship with that person—but ended up regretting the action's unexpected negative consequences for the team. Grasping this notion can be especially difficult for up-and-comers who have been able to accomplish a great deal on their own.

When new managers focus solely on one-on-one relationships, they neglect a fundamental aspect of effective leadership: harnessing the collective power of the group to improve individual performance and commitment. By shaping team culture—the group's norms and values—a leader can unleash the problem-solving prowess of the diverse talents that make up the team.

MANAGERS MUST ENSURE THAT THINGS RUN SMOOTHLY

Like many managerial myths, this one is partly true but is misleading because it tells only some of the story. Making sure an operation is operating smoothly is an incredibly difficult task, requiring a manager to keep countless balls in the air at all times. Indeed, the complexity of maintaining the status quo can absorb all of a junior manager's time and energy.

But new managers also need to realize they are responsible for recommending and initiating changes that will enhance their groups' performance. Often—and it comes as a surprise to most—this means challenging organizational processes or structures that exist above and beyond their area of formal authority. Only when they understand this part of the job will they begin to address seriously their leadership responsibilities.

(See the insert "Oh, One More Thing: Create the Conditions for Your Success" at the end of this article.)

In fact, most new managers see themselves as targets of organizational change initiatives, implementing with their groups the changes ordered from above. They don't see themselves as change agents. Hierarchical thinking and their fixation on the authority that comes with being the boss lead them to define their responsibilities too narrowly. Consequently, they tend to blame flawed systems, and the superiors directly responsible for those systems, for their teams' setbacks—and they tend to wait for other people to fix the problems.

But this represents a fundamental misunderstanding of their role within the organization. New managers need to generate changes, both within *and outside* their areas of responsibility, to ensure that their teams can succeed. They need to work to change the context in which their teams operate, ignoring their lack of formal authority.

This broader view benefits the organization as well as the new manager. Organizations must continually revitalize and transform themselves. They can meet these challenges only if they have cadres of effective leaders capable of both managing the complexity of the status quo and initiating change.

New Managers Aren't Alone

As they go through the daunting process of becoming a boss, new managers can gain a tremendous advantage by learning to recognize the misconceptions I've just outlined. But given the multilayered nature of their new responsibilities, they are still going to make mistakes as they try to put together the managerial puzzle—and making mistakes, no matter how important to the learning process, is no fun. They are going to feel pain as their professional identities are stretched and reshaped. As they struggle to learn a new role, they will often feel isolated.

Unfortunately, my research has shown that few new managers ask for help. This is in part the outcome of yet another misconception: The boss is supposed to have all the answers, so seeking help is a sure sign that a new manager is a "promotion mistake." Of course, seasoned managers know that no one has all the answers. The insights a manager does possess come over time, through experience. And, as countless studies show, it is easier to learn on the job if you can draw on the support and assistance of peers and superiors.

Another reason new managers don't seek help is that they perceive the dangers (sometimes more imagined than real) of forging developmental relationships. When you share your anxieties, mistakes, and shortcomings with peers in your part of the organization, there's a risk that the individuals will use that information against you. The same goes for sharing your problems with your superior. The inherent conflict between the roles of evaluator and developer is an age-old dilemma. So new managers need to be creative in finding support. For instance, they might seek out peers who are outside their region or function or in another organization altogether. The problem with bosses, while difficult to solve neatly, can be alleviated. And herein lies a lesson not only for new managers but for experienced bosses, as well.

The new manager avoids turning to her immediate superior for advice because she sees that person as a threat to, rather than an ally in, her development. Because she fears punishment for missteps and failures, she resists seeking the help that might prevent such mistakes, even when she's desperate for it. As one new manager reports:

"I know on one level that I should deal more with my manager because that is what he is there for. He's got the experience, and I probably owe it to him to go to him and tell him what's up. He would probably have some good advice. But it's not safe to share with him. He's an unknown quantity. If you ask too many questions, he may lose confidence in you and think things aren't going very well. He may see that you are a little bit out of control, and then you really have a tough job. Because he'll be down there lickety-split, asking lots of questions about what you are doing, and before you know it, he'll be involved right in the middle of it. That's a really uncomfortable situation. He's the last place I'd go for help."

Such fears are often justified. Many a new manager has regretted trying to establish a mentoring relationship with his boss. "I don't dare even ask a question that could be perceived as naive or stupid," says one. "Once I asked him a question and he made me feel like I was a kindergartner in the business. It was as if he had said, 'That was the dumbest thing I've ever seen. What on earth did you have in mind?'"

This is a tragically lost opportunity for the new manager, the boss, and the organization as a whole. It means that the new manager's boss loses a chance to influence the manager's initial conceptions and misconceptions of her new position and how she should approach it. The new manager loses the chance to draw on organizational assets—from financial resources to information about senior management's priorities—that the superior could best provide.

When a new manager can develop a good relationship with his boss, it can make all the difference in the world—though not necessarily in ways the new manager expects. My research suggests that eventually about half of new managers turn to their bosses for assistance, often because of a looming crisis. Many are relieved to find their superiors more tolerant of their questions and mistakes than they had expected. "He recognized that I was still in the learning mode and was more than willing to help in any way he could," recalls one new manager.

Sometimes, the most expert mentors can seem deceptively hands-off. One manager reports how she learned from an immediate superior: "She is demanding, but she enjoys a reputation for growing people and helping them, not throwing them to the wolves. I wasn't sure after the first 60 days, though. Everything was so hard and I was so frustrated, but she didn't offer to help. It was driving me nuts. When I asked her a question, she asked me a question. I got no answers. Then I saw what she wanted. I had to come in with some ideas about how I would handle the situation, and then she would talk about them with me. She would spend all the time in the world with me."

His experience vividly highlights why it's important for the bosses of new managers to understand—or simply recall—how difficult it is to step into a management role for the first time. Helping a new manager succeed doesn't benefit only that individual. Ensuring the new manager's success is also crucially important to the success of the entire organization.

Oh, One More Thing: Create the Conditions for Your Success

NEW MANAGERS OFTEN discover, belatedly, that they are expected to do more than just make sure their groups function smoothly today. They must also recommend and initiate changes that will help their groups do even better in the future.

A new marketing manager at a telecommunications company whom I'll call John Delhorne discovered that his predecessor had failed to make critical investments, so he tried on numerous occasions to convince his immediate superior to increase the marketing budget. He also presented a proposal to acquire a new information system that could allow his team to optimize its marketing initiatives. When he could not persuade his boss to release more money, he hunkered down and focused on changes within his team that would make it as productive as possible under the circumstances. This course seemed prudent, especially because his relationship with his boss, who was taking longer and longer to answer Delhorne's e-mails, was becoming strained.

When the service failed to meet certain targets, the CEO unceremoniously fired Delhorne because, Delhorne was told, he hadn't been proactive. The CEO chastised Delhorne for "sitting back and not asking for his help" in securing the funds needed to succeed in a critical new market. Delhorne, shocked and hurt, thought the CEO was being grossly unfair. Delhorne contended it wasn't his fault that the company's strategic-planning and budgeting procedures were flawed. The CEO's response: It was Delhorne's responsibility to create the conditions for his success.

Originally published in January 2007
Reprint R0701D

Discovering Your Authentic Leadership

BILL GEORGE, PETER SIMS, ANDREW N. MCLEAN, AND DIANA MAYER

Executive Summary

THE ONGOING PROBLEMS in business leadership over the past five years have underscored the need for a new kind of leader in the twenty-first century: the authentic leader. Author Bill George, a Harvard Business School professor and the former chairman and CEO of Medtronic, and his colleagues, conducted the largest leadership development study ever undertaken. They interviewed 125 business leaders from different racial, religious, national, and socioeconomic backgrounds to understand how leaders become and remain authentic. Their interviews showed that you do not have to be born with any particular characteristics or traits to lead. You also do not have to be at the top of your organization. Anyone can learn to be an authentic leader.

The journey begins with leaders understanding their life stories. Authentic leaders frame their stories in ways that allow them to see themselves not as passive observers but as individuals who learn from their experiences. These leaders make time to examine their experiences and to reflect on them, and in doing so they grow as individuals and as leaders. Authentic leaders also work hard at developing self-awareness through persistent and often courageous self-exploration. Denial can be the greatest hurdle that leaders face in becoming self-aware, but authentic leaders ask for, and listen to, honest feedback. They also use formal and informal support networks to help them stay grounded and lead integrated lives.

The authors argue that achieving business results over a sustained period of time is the ultimate mark of authentic leadership. It may be possible to drive short-term outcomes without being authentic, but authentic leadership is the only way to create long-term results.

DURING THE PAST 50 YEARS, leadership scholars have conducted more than 1,000 studies in an attempt to determine the definitive styles, characteristics, or personality traits of great leaders. None of these studies has produced a clear profile of the ideal leader. Thank goodness. If scholars had produced a cookie-cutter leadership style, individuals would be forever trying to imitate it. They would make themselves into personae, not people, and others would see through them immediately.

No one can be authentic by trying to imitate someone else. You can learn from others' experiences, but there is no way you can be successful when you are trying to be like them. People trust you when you are genuine and authentic, not a replica of someone else. Amgen CEO and president Kevin Sharer, who gained priceless experience working as Jack Welch's assistant in the 1980s, saw the downside of GE's cult of personality in those days. "Everyone wanted to be like Jack," he explains. "Leadership has many voices. You need to be who you are, not try to emulate somebody else."

Over the past five years, people have developed a deep distrust of leaders. It is increasingly evident that we need a new kind of business leader in the twenty-first century. In 2003, Bill George's book, *Authentic Leadership: Rediscovering the Secrets to Creating Lasting Value,* challenged a new generation to lead authentically. Authentic leaders demonstrate a passion for their purpose, practice their values consistently, and lead with their hearts as well as their heads. They establish long-term, meaningful relationships and have the self-discipline to get results. They know who they are.

Many readers of *Authentic Leadership,* including several CEOs, indicated that they had a tremendous desire to become authentic leaders and wanted to know how. As a result, our research team set out to answer the question, "How can people become and remain authentic leaders?" We interviewed 125 leaders to learn how they developed their leadership abilities. These interviews constitute the largest in-depth study of leadership development ever undertaken. Our interviewees discussed openly and honestly how they realized their potential and candidly shared their life stories, personal struggles, failures, and triumphs.

The people we talked with ranged in age from 23 to 93, with no fewer than 15 per decade. They were chosen based on their reputations for authenticity and effectiveness as leaders, as well as our personal knowledge of them. We also solicited recommendations from other leaders and academics. The resulting group includes women and men from a diverse array of racial, religious, and socioeconomic backgrounds and nationalities. Half of them are CEOs, and the other half comprises a range of profit and nonprofit leaders, midcareer leaders, and young leaders just starting on their journeys.

After interviewing these individuals, we believe we understand why more than 1,000 studies have not produced a profile of an ideal leader. Analyzing 3,000 pages of transcripts, our team was startled to see that these people did not identify any universal characteristics, traits, skills, or styles that led to their success. Rather, their leadership emerged from their life stories. Consciously and subconsciously, they were constantly testing themselves through real-world experiences and reframing their life stories to understand who they were at their core. In doing so, they discovered the purpose of their leadership and learned that being authentic made them more effective.

These findings are extremely encouraging: You do not have to be born with specific characteristics or traits of a leader. You do not have to wait for a tap on the shoulder. You do not have to be at the top of your organization. Instead, you can discover your potential right now. As one of our interviewees, Young & Rubicam chairman and CEO Ann Fudge, said, "All of us have the spark of leadership in us, whether it is in business, in government, or as a nonprofit volunteer. The challenge is to understand ourselves well enough to discover where we can use our leadership gifts to serve others."

Discovering your authentic leadership requires a commitment to developing yourself. Like musicians and athletes, you must devote yourself to a lifetime of realizing your potential. Most people Kroger CEO David Dillon has seen become good leaders were self-taught. Dillon said, "The advice I give to individuals in our company is not to expect the company to hand you a development plan. You need to take responsibility for developing yourself."

In the following pages, we draw upon lessons from our interviews to describe how people become authentic leaders. First and most important, they frame their life stories in ways that allow them to see themselves not as passive observers of their lives but rather as individuals who can develop self-awareness from their experiences. Authentic leaders act on that awareness by practicing their values and principles, sometimes at substantial risk to themselves. They are careful to balance their motivations so that they are driven by these inner values as much as by a desire for external rewards or recognition. Authentic leaders also keep a strong support team around them, ensuring that they live integrated, grounded lives.

Learning from Your Life Story

The journey to authentic leadership begins with understanding the story of your life. Your life story provides the context for your experiences, and through it, you can find the inspiration to make an impact in the world. As the novelist John Barth once wrote, "The story of your life is not your life. It is your story." In other words, it is your personal narrative that matters, not the mere facts of your life. Your life narrative is like a permanent recording playing in your head. Over and over, you replay the events and personal interactions that are important to your life, attempting to make sense of them to find your place in the world.

While the life stories of authentic leaders cover the full spectrum of experiences—including the positive impact of parents, athletic coaches, teachers, and mentors—many leaders reported that their motivation came from a difficult experience in their lives. They described the transformative effects of the loss of a job; personal illness; the untimely death of a close friend or relative; and feelings of being excluded, discriminated against, and rejected by peers. Rather than seeing themselves as victims, though, authentic leaders used these formative experiences to give meaning to their lives. They reframed these events to rise above their challenges and to discover their passion to lead.

Let's focus now on one leader in particular, Novartis chairman and CEO Daniel Vasella, whose life story was one of the most difficult of all the people we interviewed. He emerged from extreme challenges in his youth to reach the pinnacle of the global pharmaceutical industry, a trajectory that illustrates the trials many leaders have to go through on their journeys to authentic leadership.

Vasella was born in 1953 to a modest family in Fribourg, Switzerland. His early years were filled with medical problems that stoked his passion to become a physician. His first recollections were of a hospital where he was admitted at age four when he suffered from food poisoning. Falling ill with asthma at age five, he was sent alone to the mountains of eastern Switzerland for two summers. He found the four-month separations from his parents especially difficult because his caretaker had an alcohol problem and was unresponsive to his needs.

At age eight, Vasella had tuberculosis, followed by meningitis, and was sent to a sanatorium for a year. Lonely and homesick, he suffered a great deal that year, as his parents rarely visited him. He still remembers the pain and fear when the nurses held him down during the lumbar punctures so that he would not move. One day, a new physician arrived and took time to explain each step of the procedure. Vasella asked the doctor if he could hold a nurse's hand rather than being held down. "The amazing thing is that this time the procedure didn't hurt," Vasella recalls. "Afterward, the doctor asked me, 'How was that?' I reached up and gave him a big hug. These human gestures of forgiveness, caring, and compassion made a deep impression on me and on the kind of person I wanted to become."

Throughout his early years, Vasella's life continued to be unsettled. When he was ten, his 18-year-old sister passed away after suffering from cancer for two years. Three years later, his father died in surgery. To support the family, his mother went to work in a distant town and came home only once every three weeks. Left to himself, he and his friends held beer parties and got into frequent fights. This lasted for three years until he met his first girlfriend, whose affection changed his life.

At 20, Vasella entered medical school, later graduating with honors. During medical school, he sought out psychotherapy so he could come to terms with his early experiences and not feel like a victim. Through analysis, he reframed his life story and realized that he wanted to help a wider range of people than he could as an individual practitioner. Upon completion of his residency, he applied to become chief physician at the University of Zurich; however, the search committee considered him too young for the position.

Disappointed but not surprised, Vasella decided to use his abilities to increase his impact on medicine. At that time, he had a growing fascination with finance and business. He talked with the head of the pharmaceutical division of Sandoz, who offered him the opportunity to join the company's U.S. affiliate. In his five years in the United States, Vasella flourished in the stimulating environment, first as a sales representative and later as a product manager, and advanced rapidly through the Sandoz marketing organization.

When Sandoz merged with Ciba-Geigy in 1996, Vasella was named CEO of the combined companies, now called Novartis, despite his young age and limited experience. Once in the CEO's role, Vasella blossomed as a leader. He envisioned the opportunity to build a great global health care company that could help people through lifesaving new drugs, such as Gleevec, which has proved to be highly effective for patients with chronic myeloid leukemia. Drawing on the physician role models of his youth, he built an entirely new Novartis culture centered on compassion, competence, and competition. These moves established Novartis as a giant in the industry and Vasella as a compassionate leader.

Vasella's experience is just one of dozens provided by authentic leaders who traced their inspiration directly from their life stories. Asked what empowered them to lead, these leaders consistently replied that they found their strength through transformative experiences. Those experiences enabled them to understand the deeper purpose of their leadership.

Knowing Your Authentic Self

When the 75 members of Stanford Graduate School of Business's Advisory Council were asked to recommend the most important capability for leaders to develop, their answer was nearly unanimous: self-awareness. Yet many leaders, especially those early in their careers, are trying so hard to establish themselves in the world that they leave little time for self-exploration. They strive to achieve success in tangible ways that are recognized in the external world—money, fame, power, status, or a rising stock price. Often their drive enables them to be professionally successful for a while, but they are unable to sustain that success. As they age, they may find something is missing in their lives and realize they are holding back from being the person they want to be. Knowing their authentic selves requires the courage and honesty to open up and examine their experiences. As they do so, leaders become more humane and willing to be vulnerable.

Of all the leaders we interviewed, David Pottruck, former CEO of Charles Schwab, had one of the most persistent journeys to self-awareness. An all-league football player in high school, Pottruck became MVP of his college team at the University of Pennsylvania. After completing his MBA at Wharton and a stint with Citigroup, he joined Charles Schwab as head of marketing, moving from New York to San Francisco. An extremely hard worker, Pottruck could not understand why his new colleagues resented the long hours he put in and his aggressiveness in pushing for results. "I thought my accomplishments would speak for themselves," he said. "It never occurred to me that my level of energy would intimidate and offend other people, because in my mind I was trying to help the company."

Pottruck was shocked when his boss told him, "Dave, your colleagues do not trust you." As he recalled, "That feedback was like a dagger to my heart. I was in denial, as I didn't see myself as others saw me. I became a lightning rod for friction, but I had no idea how self-serving I looked to other people. Still, somewhere in my inner core the feedback resonated as true." Pottruck realized that he could not succeed unless he identified and overcame his blind spots.

Denial can be the greatest hurdle that leaders face in becoming self-aware. They all have egos that need to be stroked, insecurities that need to be smoothed, fears that need to be allayed. Authentic leaders realize that they have to be willing to listen to feedback—especially the kind they don't want to hear. It was only after his second divorce that Pottruck finally was able to acknowledge that he still had large blind spots: "After my second marriage fell apart, I thought I had a wife-selection problem." Then he worked with a counselor who delivered some hard truths: "The good news is you do not have a wife-selection problem; the bad news is you have a husband-behavior problem." Pottruck then made a determined effort to change. As he described it, "I was like a guy who has had three heart attacks and finally realizes he has to quit smoking and lose some weight."

These days Pottruck is happily remarried and listens carefully when his wife offers constructive feedback. He acknowledges that he falls back on his old habits at times, particularly in high stress situations, but now he has developed ways of coping with stress. "I have had enough success in life to have that foundation of self-respect, so I can take the criticism and not deny it. I have finally learned to tolerate my failures and disappointments and not beat myself up."

Practicing Your Values and Principles

The values that form the basis for authentic leadership are derived from your beliefs and convictions, but you will not know what your true values are until they are tested under pressure. It is relatively easy to list your values and to live by them when things are going well. When your success, your career, or even your life hangs in the balance, you learn what is most important, what you are prepared to sacrifice, and what trade-offs you are willing to make.

Leadership principles are values translated into action. Having a solid base of values and testing them under fire enables you to develop the principles you will use in leading. For example, a value such as "concern for others" might be translated into a leadership principle such as "create a work environment where people are respected for their contributions, provided job security, and allowed to fulfill their potential."

Consider Jon Huntsman, the founder and chairman of Huntsman Corporation. His moral values were deeply challenged when he worked for the Nixon administration in 1972, shortly before Watergate. After a brief stint in the U.S. Department of Health, Education, and Welfare (HEW), he took a job under H.R. Haldeman, President Nixon's powerful chief of staff. Huntsman said he found the experience of taking orders from Haldeman "very mixed. I wasn't geared to take orders, irrespective of whether they were ethically or morally right." He explained, "We had a few clashes, as plenty of things that Haldeman wanted to do were questionable. An amoral atmosphere permeated the White House."

One day, Haldeman directed Huntsman to help him entrap a California congressman who had been opposing a White House initiative. The congressman was part owner of a plant that reportedly employed undocumented workers. To gather information to embarrass the congressman, Haldeman told Huntsman to get the plant manager of a company Huntsman owned to place some undocumented workers at the congressman's plant in an undercover operation.

"There are times when we react too quickly and fail to realize immediately what is right and wrong," Huntsman recalled. "This was one of those times when I didn't think it through. I knew instinctively it was wrong, but it took a few minutes for the notion to percolate. After 15 minutes, my inner moral compass made itself noticed and enabled me to recognize this wasn't the right thing to do. Values that had accompanied me since childhood kicked in. Halfway through my conversation with our plant manager, I said to him, 'Let's not do this. I don't want to play this game. Forget that I called.'"

Huntsman told Haldeman that he would not use his employees in this way. "Here I was saying no to the second most powerful person in the country. He didn't appreciate responses like that, as he viewed them as signs of disloyalty. I might as well have been saying farewell. So be it. I left within the next six months."

Balancing Your Extrinsic and Intrinsic Motivations

Because authentic leaders need to sustain high levels of motivation and keep their lives in balance, it is critically important for them to understand what drives them. There are two types of motivations—extrinsic and intrinsic. Although they are reluctant to admit it, many leaders are propelled to achieve by measuring their success against the outside world's parameters. They enjoy the recognition and status that come with promotions and financial rewards. Intrinsic motivations, on the other hand, are derived from their sense of the meaning of their life. They are closely linked to one's life story and the way one frames it. Examples include personal growth, helping other people develop, taking on social causes, and making a difference in the world. The key is to find a balance between your desires for external validation and the intrinsic motivations that provide fulfillment in your work.

Many interviewees advised aspiring leaders to be wary of getting caught up in social, peer, or parental expectations. Debra Dunn, who has worked in Silicon Valley for decades as a Hewlett-Packard executive, acknowledged the constant pressures from external sources: "The path of accumulating material possessions is clearly laid out. You know how to measure it. If you don't pursue that path, people wonder what is wrong with you. The only way to avoid getting caught up in materialism is to understand where you find happiness and fulfillment."

Moving away from the external validation of personal achievement is not always easy. Achievement-oriented leaders grow so accustomed to successive accomplishments throughout their early years that it takes courage to pursue their intrinsic motivations. But at some point, most leaders recognize that they need to address more difficult questions in order to pursue truly meaningful success. McKinsey's Alice Woodwark, who at 29 has already achieved notable success, reflected: "My version of achievement was pretty naive, born of things I learned early in life about praise and being valued. But if you're just chasing the rabbit around the course, you're not running toward anything meaningful."

Intrinsic motivations are congruent with your values and are more fulfilling than extrinsic motivations. John Thain, CEO of the New York Stock Exchange, said, "I am motivated by doing a really good job at whatever I am doing, but I prefer to multiply my impact on society through a group of people." Or as Ann Moore, chairman and CEO of Time, put it, "I came here 25 years ago solely because I loved magazines and the publishing world." Moore had a dozen job offers after business school but took the lowest-paying one with Time because of her passion for publishing.

Building Your Support Team

Leaders cannot succeed on their own; even the most outwardly confident executives need support and advice. Without strong relationships to provide perspective, it is very easy to lose your way.

Authentic leaders build extraordinary support teams to help them stay on course. Those teams counsel them in times of uncertainty, help them in times of difficulty, and celebrate with them in times of success. After their hardest days, leaders find comfort in being with people on whom they can rely so they can be open and vulnerable. During the low points, they cherish the friends who appreciate them for who they are, not what they are. Authentic leaders find that their support teams provide affirmation, advice, perspective, and calls for course corrections when needed.

How do you go about building your support team? Most authentic leaders have a multifaceted support structure that includes their spouses or significant others, families, mentors, close friends, and colleagues. They build their networks over time, as the experiences, shared histories, and openness with people close to them create the trust and confidence they need in times of trial and uncertainty. Leaders must give as much to their supporters as they get from them so that mutually beneficial relationships can develop.

It starts with having at least one person in your life with whom you can be completely yourself, warts and all, and still be accepted unconditionally. Often that person is the only one who can tell you the honest truth. Most leaders have their closest relationships with their spouses, although some develop these bonds with another family member, a close friend, or a trusted mentor. When leaders can rely on unconditional support, they are more likely to accept themselves for who they really are.

Many relationships grow over time through an expression of shared values and a common purpose. Randy Komisar of venture capital firm Kleiner Perkins Caufield & Byers said his marriage to Hewlett-Packard's Debra Dunn is lasting because it is rooted in similar values. "Debra and I are very independent but extremely harmonious in terms of our personal aspirations, values, and principles. We have a strong resonance around questions like, 'What is your legacy in this world?' It is important to be in sync about what we do with our lives."

Many leaders have had a mentor who changed their lives. The best mentoring interactions spark mutual learning, exploration of similar values, and shared enjoyment. If people are only looking for a leg up from their mentors, instead of being interested in their mentors' lives as well, the relationships will not last for long. It is the two-way nature of the connection that sustains it.

Personal and professional support groups can take many forms. Piper Jaffray's Tad Piper is a member of an

Alcoholics Anonymous group. He noted, "These are not CEOs. They are just a group of nice, hard-working people who are trying to stay sober, lead good lives, and work with each other about being open, honest, and vulnerable. We reinforce each other's behavior by talking about our chemical dependency in a disciplined way as we go through the 12 steps. I feel blessed to be surrounded by people who are thinking about those kinds of issues and actually doing something, not just talking about them."

Bill George's experiences echo Piper's: In 1974, he joined a men's group that formed after a weekend retreat. More than 30 years later, the group is still meeting every Wednesday morning. After an opening period of catching up on each other's lives and dealing with any particular difficulty someone may be facing, one of the group's eight members leads a discussion on a topic he has selected. These discussions are open, probing, and often profound. The key to their success is that people say what they really believe without fear of judgment, criticism, or reprisal. All the members consider the group to be one of the most important aspects of their lives, enabling them to clarify their beliefs, values, and understanding of vital issues, as well as serving as a source of honest feedback when they need it most.

Integrating Your Life by Staying Grounded

Integrating their lives is one of the greatest challenges leaders face. To lead a balanced life, you need to bring together all of its constituent elements—work, family, community, and friends—so that you can be the same person in each environment. Think of your life as a house, with a bedroom for your personal life, a study for your professional life, a family room for your family, and a living room to share with your friends. Can you knock down the walls between these rooms and be the same person in each of them?

As John Donahoe, president of eBay Marketplaces and former worldwide managing director of Bain, stressed, being authentic means maintaining a sense of self no matter where you are. He warned, "The world can shape you if you let it. To have a sense of yourself as you live, you must make conscious choices. Sometimes the choices are really hard, and you make a lot of mistakes."

Authentic leaders have a steady and confident presence. They do not show up as one person one day and another person the next. Integration takes discipline, particularly during stressful times when it is easy to become reactive and slip back into bad habits. Donahoe feels strongly that integrating his life has enabled him to become a more effective leader. "There is no nirvana," he said. "The struggle is constant, as the trade-offs don't get any easier as you get older." But for authentic leaders, personal and professional lives are not a zero-sum game. As Donahoe said, "I have no doubt today that my children have made me a far more effective leader in the workplace. Having a strong personal life has made the difference."

Leading is high-stress work. There is no way to avoid stress when you are responsible for people, organizations, outcomes, and managing the constant uncertainties of the environment. The higher you go, the greater your freedom to control your destiny but also the higher the degree of stress. The question is not whether you can avoid stress but how you can control it to maintain your own sense of equilibrium.

Authentic leaders are constantly aware of the importance of staying grounded. Besides spending time with their families and close friends, authentic leaders get physical exercise, engage in spiritual practices, do community service, and return to the places where they grew up. All are essential to their effectiveness as leaders, enabling them to sustain their authenticity.

Empowering People to Lead

Now that we have discussed the process of discovering your authentic leadership, let's look at how authentic leaders empower people in their organizations to achieve superior long-term results, which is the bottom line for all leaders.

Authentic leaders recognize that leadership is not about their success or about getting loyal subordinates to follow them. They know the key to a successful organization is having empowered leaders at all levels, including those who have no direct reports. They not only inspire those around them, they empower those individuals to step up and lead.

A reputation for building relationships and empowering people was instrumental in chairman and CEO Anne Mulcahy's stunning turnaround of Xerox. When Mulcahy was asked to take the company's reins from her failed predecessor, Xerox had $18 billion in debt, and all credit lines were exhausted. With the share price in free fall, morale was at an all-time low. To make matters worse, the SEC was investigating the company's revenue recognition practices.

Mulcahy's appointment came as a surprise to everyone—including Mulcahy herself. A Xerox veteran, she had worked in field sales and on the corporate staff for 25 years, but not in finance, R&D, or manufacturing. How could Mulcahy cope with this crisis when she had

had no financial experience? She brought to the CEO role the relationships she had built over 25 years, an impeccable understanding of the organization, and, above all, her credibility as an authentic leader. She bled for Xerox, and everyone knew it. Because of that, they were willing to go the extra mile for her.

After her appointment, Mulcahy met personally with the company's top 100 executives to ask them if they would stay with the company despite the challenges ahead. "I knew there were people who weren't supportive of me," she said. "So I confronted a couple of them and said, 'This is about the company.'" The first two people Mulcahy talked with, both of whom ran big operating units, decided to leave, but the remaining 98 committed to stay.

Throughout the crisis, people in Xerox were empowered by Mulcahy to step up and lead in order to restore the company to its former greatness. In the end, her leadership enabled Xerox to avoid bankruptcy as she paid back $10 billion in debt and restored revenue growth and profitability with a combination of cost savings and innovative new products. The stock price tripled as a result.

Like Mulcahy, all leaders have to deliver bottom-line results. By creating a virtuous circle in which the results reinforce the effectiveness of their leadership, authentic leaders are able to sustain those results through good times and bad. Their success enables them to attract talented people and align employees' activities with shared goals, as they empower others on their team to lead by taking on greater challenges. Indeed, superior results over a sustained period of time is the ultimate mark of an authentic leader. It may be possible to drive short-term outcomes without being authentic, but authentic leadership is the only way we know to create sustainable long-term results.

For authentic leaders, there are special rewards. No individual achievement can equal the pleasure of leading a group of people to achieve a worthy goal. When you cross the finish line together, all the pain and suffering you may have experienced quickly vanishes. It is replaced by a deep inner satisfaction that you have empowered others and thus made the world a better place. That's the challenge and the fulfillment of authentic leadership.

Your Development as an Authentic Leader

AS YOU READ this article, think about the basis for your leadership development and the path you need to follow to become an authentic leader. Then ask yourself these questions:

1. **Which people and experiences in your early life had the greatest impact on you?**
2. **What tools do you use to become self-aware?** What is your authentic self? What are the moments when you say to yourself, this is the real me?
3. **What are your most deeply held values?** Where did they come from? Have your values changed significantly since your childhood? How do your values inform your actions?
4. **What motivates you extrinsically?** What are your intrinsic motivations? How do you balance extrinsic and intrinsic motivation in your life?

5. **What kind of support team do you have?** How can your support team make you a more authentic leader? How should you diversify your team to broaden your perspective?
6. **Is your life integrated?** Are you able to be the same person in all aspects of your life—personal, work, family, and community? If not, what is holding you back?
7. **What does being authentic mean in your life?** Are you more effective as a leader when you behave authentically? Have you ever paid a price for your authenticity as a leader? Was it worth it?
8. **What steps can you take today, tomorrow, and over the next year to develop your authentic leadership?**

Originally published in February 2007
Reprint R0702H

About the Contributors

KERRY A. BUNKER AND SHARON TING are managers of the Awareness Program for Executive Excellence at the Center for Creative Leadership in Greensboro, North Carolina.

JOHN J. GABARRO is the UPS Foundation Professor of Human Resource Management in Organizational Behavior at Harvard Business School in Boston.

BILL GEORGE, former Chairman and CEO of Medtronic, is now a professor of management practice at Harvard Business School in Boston.

NATALIE SHOPE GRIFFIN is a consultant in executive and organizational development at Nationwide Financial, a financial services company based in Columbus, OH.

ROBERT HANIG is a vice president of Dialogos in Cambridge, Massachusetts.

LINDA A. HILL is the Wallace Brett Donham Professor of Business Administration at Harvard Business School in Boston.

KATHY E. KRAM is a professor of organizational behavior at the Boston University School of Management.

J. STERLING LIVINGSTON was formerly a professor of business administration at the Harvard Business School.

DIANA MAYER is a former Citigroup executive in New York.

ANDREW N. MCLEAN is a research assistant at Harvard Business School.

ANDREAS PRIESTLAND is a senior consultant for organizational development at London-based BP.

PETER SIMS established "Leadership Perspectives," a class on leadership development at the Stanford Graduate School of Business in California.

CAROL A. WALKER is the President of Prepared to Lead, a management consulting firm in Weston, Massachusetts.

Index